POWERS OF ATTORNEY: A STATUTORY ANNOTATION

POWERS OF ATTORNEY: A STATUTORY ANNOTATION

(Fourth Edition)

Brian Gallagher

B.C.L., Solicitor

with

Niamh O'Herlihy

ROUND HALL

THOMSON REUTERS

Published in 2016 by
Thomson Reuters Ireland Limited
(Registered in Ireland, Company No. 416940.
Registered Office and address for service:
43 Fitzwilliam Place, Dublin 2, Ireland)
trading as Round Hall

Typeset by
Gough Typesetting Services
Dublin

Printed by
CPI Group (UK) Ltd, Croydon, CR0 477

ISBN 978-0-41405-988-7

A catalogue record for this book
is available from the British Library

Table of Contents

PART 1

POWERS OF ATTORNEY ACT 1996 AS AMENDED

PART 1

POWERS OF ATTORNEY ACT 1996 AS AMENDED

INTRODUCTION

The purpose of this book is to show comprehensively the Powers of Attorney Act 1996 (the "1996 Act") as amended by all legislation, up to and including the Assisted Decision-Making (Capacity) Act 2015 (the "2015 Act"). Because of the manner in which the 2015 Act amended the 1996 Act, it is necessary to reproduce, in Part 1 of this book, the 1996 Act as amended prior to the commencement of the 2015 Act, and, in Part 2, the legislation relating to Enduring Powers of Attorney after the coming into force of the 2015 Act.

Part 1, therefore, deals with the legislation currently in force relating to ordinary Powers of Attorney, and with the legislation concerning Enduring Powers of Attorney created under the provisions of the 1996 Act. Part 2 deals with the legislation concerning Enduring Powers of Attorney created after the commencement of the 2015 Act. Enduring Powers of Attorney created under the provisions of the 1996 Act in force up to the commencement of the 2015 Act are not affected by the 2015 Act, except insofar as is provided by s.81 of the 2015 Act.

Practitioners should be aware of the differences between Enduring Powers of Attorney created under the provisions of the 1996 Act and those created under the provisions of the 2015 Act. The latter provide for the better safeguarding of the Donor, although they are more onerous administratively.

POWERS OF ATTORNEY ACT 1996

(1996 No. 12)

ARRANGEMENT OF SECTIONS

PART I

PRELIMINARY AND GENERAL

PART II

ENDURING POWERS OF ATTORNEY

PART III

POWERS OF ATTORNEY GENERALLY

An Act to provide for powers of attorney to operate when the donor of the power is or is becoming mentally incapable and to amend in other respects the law relating to powers of attorney generally. [*5th June*, 1996]

Introduction and General Note

The object of this legislation was twofold: first, to provide for what was in 1996 in Ireland a new legal creature called "an enduring power", a power of attorney which, with certain exceptions, comes into force when it has been registered under s.10 of the Act, and is not revoked by the donor's subsequent mental incapacity; and secondly, to make certain amendments to the law relating to powers of attorney generally.

It was not possible to create an instrument with the characteristics of an enduring power prior to the commencement of the 1996 Act. The commonly understood power of attorney came (and still comes) into effect on execution, and lasts (and continues to last) until death, revocation or the onset of mental incapacity. The problem with the commonly known power of attorney was (and is) that it ceases to have effect when the donor becomes mentally incapable. Both the enduring power and the commonly known power of attorney cease on the death of a donor.

Enduring powers are a phenomenon of the late twentieth century. They were introduced in England and Wales by the Enduring Powers of Attorney Act 1995 (c.29), replaced by lasting powers of attorney when the Mental Capacity Act 2005 came into operation on 1 October 2007, and are provided for in many other common law jurisdictions, for example, in the United States of America, Canada, Australia and New Zealand. For those interested in a detailed study of enduring powers, working papers or reports have been issued by the Law Reform Commissions of, for example, Ontario, British Columbia, Australia, Manitoba and Newfoundland, quite apart from the work which has been done by the UK Law Commission. For a detailed discussion on enduring powers, see the Law Reform Commission's Consultation Paper on *Law and the Elderly* (CP23–2003) and its Consultation Paper and Report on *Vulnerable Adults and the Law* (CP33–2005 and LRC Report 83–2006). The Government is planning to introduce a Mental Capacity Bill to implement the recommendations of the latter Report. A Scheme for this Bill is published on the Department of Justice, Equality and Law Reform's website dated September 5, 2008. See also, Anne Marie O'Neill, *Irish Mental Health Law* (Dublin: First Law, 2005), pp.549 and following.

The Powers of Attorney Bill 1995 was initially introduced in Seanad Éireann when the Minister for Equality and Law Reform stated that it was:

> "An important social measure, the purpose of which is to allow persons to put in place arrangements for managing their affairs in the event that they should become mentally disabled." (144 *Seanad Debates* Col.1241.)

In restating the law as it existed at that time, he said that:

> "When a person becomes mentally incapable and the question of managing his or her affairs arises, the only option under the existing law is to have that person made a ward of court. Wardship can be a complex, time-consuming and expensive procedure." (144 *Seanad Debates* Col.1241.)

The wards of court jurisdiction of the courts is not affected in any way by the Act.

The Minister referred to the incidence of Alzheimer's disease, stating that it was believed that there are more than 25,000 Irish *adult* sufferers, who may be as young as 50, 40, or even 30 years of age. Concluding his opening comments, the Minister stated that:

> "Mental incapacity can also result from brain injury at any age, perhaps most commonly from road accidents. The existence of a power of attorney which would not be revoked on the occurrence of mental incapacity would act as a kind of insurance against the effects of accidental injuries of this kind. In fact in jurisdictions where enduring powers of attorney have been introduced, many young people have executed these enduring powers as a precaution against such an eventuality." (144 *Seanad Debates* Col.1242.)

In dealing with Part III of the Act, the Minister said that it was "concerned with updating the law on powers of attorney generally" (144 *Seanad Debates* Col.1247). While mentioning ss.15 and 16 particularly, the Minister characterised the remaining sections in Part III as being "of a technical nature and ... best left for consideration on committee stage" (144 *Seanad Debates* Col.1247).

The Act had an uncontroversial passage through the Oireachtas, but quite a number of amendments were made to the initial Bill, necessitating its return to Seanad Éireann after passage by Dáil Éireann. Many of these amendments were brought about as a result of representations made by the Law Society of Ireland and the Dublin Solicitors Bar Association.

Commencement

The Act was signed by the President on June 5, 1996 and came into force pursuant to S.I. No. 195 of 1996 on 1 August 1996.

Statutory Instruments

Powers of Attorney Act, 1996 (Commencement) Order 1996 (S.I. No. 195 of 1996)
Enduring Powers of Attorney Regulations 1996 (S.I. No. 196 of 1996)
Enduring Powers of Attorney (Personal Care Decision) Regulations 1996 (S.I. No. 287 of 1996)
Rules of the Superior Courts (No. 1) (Powers of Attorney Act 1996), 2000 (S.I. No. 66 of 2000)

Acts Referred to

Companies Act, 1990	1990, No. 33
Conveyancing Act, 1881	1881, c. 41
Conveyancing Act, 1882	1882, c. 39
Health (Nursing Homes) Act, 1990	1990, No. 23
Lunacy Regulation (Ireland) Act, 1871	1871, c. 22
Settled Land Act, 1882	1882, c. 38
Stock Exchange Act, 1995	1995, No. 9
Stock Transfer Act, 1963	1963, No. 34
Succession Act, 1965	1965, No. 27

Be it enacted by the Oireachtas as follows:

Part I

Preliminary and General

Short title and commencement

1.—(1) This Act may be cited as the Powers of Attorney Act, 1996.

(2) This Act shall come into force on such day or days as the Minister shall appoint by order or orders either generally or with reference to any particular provisions and different days may be so fixed for different provisions.

Interpretation generally

2.—(1) In this Act, unless the context otherwise requires—

"convey" includes transfer, lease and assign, and "conveyance" shall be construed accordingly;

"power" means power of attorney;

"power of attorney" means an instrument signed by or by direction of a person (the donor), or a provision contained in such an instrument, giving the donee the power to act on behalf of the donor in accordance with the terms of the instrument;

"statutory declaration" includes a statutory declaration made in accordance with section 3.

(2)(*a*) In this Act a reference to a Part, section or Schedule is a reference to a Part, section or Schedule of this Act unless it is indicated that reference to some other enactment is intended.

(*b*) In this Act a reference to a subsection, paragraph or subparagraph is a reference to the subsection, paragraph or subparagraph of the provision in which the reference occurs unless it is indicated that reference to some other provision is intended.

(3) In this Act a reference to an Act is to that Act as subsequently amended.

General Note

Section 2 is an interpretation section for the purposes of the Act. The original definition of "power of attorney" in the Bill was amended. As originally defined, "power of attorney" meant "an instrument signed by or by direction of a person (the donor) and by the donee (or by each donee if more than one) giving the donee or donees the power to act on behalf of the donor in accordance with the terms of the instrument". The definition as originally drafted would have imposed an additional requirement in relation to *all* powers of attorney; that they be signed by the donee as well as the donor. (Enduring Powers must, however, be signed by both donor and donee.)

Prior to this enactment there were no special provisions in Ireland governing the creation of a power of attorney (ss.7 and 8 of the Conveyancing Act 1882 dealt with the irrevocability of powers of attorney). The rule at common law was that it had to be done by deed (see *R. v Martin* (1831) Glasc. 33). In the case of a corporation, the requirements of its memorandum and articles of association, e.g. in relation to affixing its seal, had to be met (see *O'Connor v Bernard* (1842) 4 Ir. Eq. R. 689).

Statutory declaration by company

3.—Where, for any purpose of this Act, a statutory declaration is to be made by a person being a corporation aggregate it may be made on behalf of the corporation by a person authorised by the corporation to act on its behalf.

General Note

Section 3 facilitates the making of statutory declarations for any purposes of the Act where the statutory declaration has to be made by a company, e.g. for the purposes of ss.13(4) or 18(4).

Part II

Enduring Powers of Attorney

General Note

This Part applies to Enduring Powers of Attorney created under the provisions of this Act only. Enduring Powers of Attorney cannot be created under this Act after the commencement of Part 7 of the Assisted Decision-Making (Capacity) Act 2015 (the "2015 Act").

Interpretation

4.—(1) In this Part—

"affairs", in relation to a donor of an enduring power, means business or financial affairs of the donor;

"attorney" means the donee of an enduring power and includes a person acting in pursuance of section 5(3) and complying with the provisions of this Act and regulations made thereunder;

"the court" means the High Court;

"enduring power" shall be construed in accordance with section 5(1);

"mental incapacity", in relation to an individual, means incapacity by reason of a mental condition to manage and administer his or her own property and affairs and cognate expressions shall be construed accordingly;

"the Minister" means the Minister for Equality and Law Reform;

"notice" means notice in writing;

"personal care decision", in relation to a donor of an enduring power, means a decision on any one or more of the following matters:

(a) where the donor should live,

(b) with whom the donor should live,

(c) whom the donor should see and not see,

(d) what training or rehabilitation the donor should get,

(e) the donor's diet and dress,

(f) inspection of the donor's personal papers,

(g) housing, social welfare and other benefits for the donor;

"registration", in relation to an enduring power of attorney, means registration under section 10, and "registered" shall be construed accordingly.

(2) An application or reference to the court under this Part shall be made in a summary manner.

(3) If any question arises under this Part as to what the donor of the enduring

power might at any time be expected to do it shall be assumed that the donor had the mental capacity to do so.

General Note

This section is an interpretation section for the purposes of Part II of the Act. Important government amendments were made to the section as originally worded in the Bill. The first amendment was the insertion of a definition of "affairs". The word "affairs" is used in s.6 (below), and the amendment was intended to restrict its interpretation. Representations had been made by, inter alia, the Law Society of Ireland and the Dublin Solicitors' Bar Association that the Act should empower the donee of an enduring power to make what are later termed "personal care decisions" on behalf of a donor. This power was not included in the Bill as introduced. It was argued that on one interpretation the word "affairs" could extend to personal care decisions. It seems, therefore, that by introducing the provision to empower a donee specifically to make certain personal care decisions, it was decided specifically to restrict the meaning of the word "affairs" to the "business or financial affairs" of the donor.

The definition of "attorney" was amended to include substitute attornies appointed under s.5(3). "The court" is defined as the High Court. There was considerable parliamentary debate in relation to this, and in particular Mr Michael Woods TD, the Fianna Fáil Spokesman on Equality and Law Reform, pressed the Minister quite strongly to change "the court" to the Circuit Court (465 *Dáil Debates* Col.1133). However, despite the arguments of the Opposition, "the court" remained as the High Court. The Act is, however, not as clear as it might be in relation to whether applications for the registration of an enduring power should be made to a judge of the High Court or to the Registrar of Wards of Court.

In a Practice Direction (see Appendix C below) which was made by the President of the High Court after the Act had come into operation, it was provided that applications for the registration of enduring powers should, in effect, be made to a Judge of the High Court, by means of the issuing of a special summons. This Practice Direction has been supplanted by S.I. No. 66 of 2000 (see Appendix D below).

In this connection, it is interesting to see that the Minister for Equality and Law Reform stated to the Dáil that registration of the enduring power would be "done in the office on an administrative basis". And "it is rather similar to the Probate application procedures" (465 *Dáil Debates* Cols 1134–1135).

The definition of "mental incapacity" as meaning "incapacity by reason of a mental condition" is now seen as being possibly problematical. A practical problem has arisen in relation to people suffering from strokes. They may suffer from very serious physical, but in many cases, not mental, incapacity.

The definition of "personal care decision" was not in the original Bill and was introduced after representations were made by, inter alia, the Law Society of Ireland and the Dublin Solicitors Bar Association. Many of those making representations sought to have the definition specifically extend to medical treatment. However, this seems to have been regarded as too much of a "hot potato" and the Act does not empower the donee to make decisions regarding the donor's medical treatment.

This legislative approach has been changed by the enactment of the 2015 Act—see ss.59 and 62 thereof in Part 2, pp.107 and 112.

Section 4(2) did not appear in the Bill as introduced. (See comments above in this note on the definition of "the court".) Section 4(3) originally contained the phrase, "unless the contrary is shown", after the word "assumed". This subsection can be connected to s.6(4) and (5) which refer to matters which the donor might be expected to do. For example, s.6(4) empowers an attorney under an enduring power to act in relation to the attorney or another person to provide for his or her or that person's needs, respectively, "if the donor might be expected" to do so. Presumably, it was thought necessary to ensure that the expectation of the donor would be looked at objectively, and not challenged subjectively on the grounds of the donor's lack of mental capacity.

Characteristics of enduring power

5.—(1) A power of attorney is an enduring power within the meaning of this Act if the instrument creating the power contains a statement by the donor to the effect that the donor intends the power to be effective during any subsequent mental incapacity of the donor and complies with the provisions of this section and regulations made thereunder.

(2) The Minister may make provision by regulations in relation to all of the following matters concerning enduring powers of attorney:

(a) their form,

(b) their execution,

(c) ensuring that any document purporting to create an enduring power incorporates adequate information as to the effect of creating or accepting the power,

(d) the inclusion in the document of all of the following statements—

(i) by the donor, that the donor has read the information as to the effect of creating the power or that such information has been read to the donor,

(ii) by a solicitor (or a member of some other specified class of persons), that, after interviewing the donor and making any necessary enquiries, the solicitor or such member—

(I) is satisfied that the donor understood the effect of creating the power, and

(II) has no reason to believe that the document is being executed by the donor as a result of fraud or undue pressure,

(iii) by a registered medical practitioner, that in his or her opinion at the time the document was executed the donor had the mental capacity, with the assistance of such explanations as may have been given to the donor, to understand the effect of creating the power,

(iv) by the attorney, that the attorney understands the duties and obligations of an attorney and the requirements of registration under section 10,

(e) the keeping of accounts by the attorney in relation to the management and disposal of the donor's property,

(f) the remuneration, if any, to be paid to the attorney,

(g) the attestation of the signatures of the donor and the attorney,

(h) specific provision for cases where more than one attorney is appointed,

(i) the giving by the donor to specified persons of notice of the execution of the power, and

(j) if the regulations amend or revoke any regulations previously made under this subsection, saving and transitional provisions.

(3) The donor of an enduring power may in the document creating the power appoint one or more specified persons, being persons who are not disqualified, to act as attorney if an attorney appointed by the power dies or is unable or declines to act or is disqualified from acting as attorney.

(4) A power of attorney cannot be an enduring power unless, when executing

the instrument creating it, the attorney is—

(a) (i) an individual who has attained 18 years and has not been adjudicated bankrupt or convicted of an offence involving fraud or dishonesty or an offence against the person or property of the donor or is not—

(I) a person in respect of whom a declaration has been made under section 150 of the Companies Act, 1990, or

(II) a person who is or was subject or deemed subject to a disqualification order by virtue of Part VII of that Act,

or

(ii) a trust corporation (within the meaning of section 30 of the Succession Act, 1965),

(b) not the owner of a nursing home (whether or not it is a nursing home within the meaning of the Health (Nursing Homes) Act, 1990) in which the donor resides, or a person residing with or an employee or agent of the owner, unless the attorney is a spouse, [or civil partner within the meaning of the Civil Partnership and Certain Rights and Obligations of Cohabitants Act 2010], parent, child or sibling of the donor.

(5) A power of attorney which gives the attorney a right to appoint a substitute or successor cannot be an enduring power.

(6) Subject to subsection (8) and sections 14(3) and 14(5), an enduring power shall be invalidated or, as the case may be, shall cease to be in force on the adjudication in bankruptcy of the attorney or, if the attorney is a body corporate, by its winding up or dissolution or on the attorney being convicted of an offence referred to in subsection (4)(a)(i) or becoming—

(a) a person referred to in clause (I) or (II) of subsection (4)(a)(i), or

(b) an owner of a nursing home or other person referred to in subsection (4)(b),

unless the attorney is an attorney appointed by the power and subsection (3) applies.

(7) An enduring power in favour of a spouse shall, unless the power provides otherwise, be invalidated or, as the case may be, cease to be in force if subsequently—

[(a) the marriage is annulled or dissolved either-

(i) under the law of the State, or

(ii) under the law of another state and is, by reason of that annulment or divorce, not or no longer a subsisting valid marriage under the law of the State,]

(b) either a decree of judicial separation is granted to either spouse by a court in the State or any decree is so granted by a court outside the State and is recognised in the State as having the like effect,

(c) a written agreement to separate is entered into between the spouses, or

(d) a protection order, interim barring order, barring order or safety order is made against the attorney on the application of the donor, or *vice versa*.

(8) Subsection (6) shall not apply to an enduring power which authorises, or

to the extent that it authorises, an attorney to make personal care decisions on behalf of the donor unless the attorney has been convicted of an offence against the person of the donor or has become a person who would be disqualified from acting as attorney by virtue of subsection (4)(b).

(9) An enduring power shall be invalidated or, as the case may be, shall cease to be in force on the exercise by the court of any of its powers under the Lunacy Regulation (Ireland) Act, 1871, if the court so directs.

(10) No disclaimer, whether by deed or otherwise, of an enduring power which has not been registered under section 10 shall be valid unless and until the attorney gives notice of it to the donor.

(11) In subsection (4)(b) "owner" includes a person managing a nursing home or a director (including a shadow director within the meaning of section 27 of the Companies Act, 1990) of, or a shareholder in, a company which owns or manages such a home.

General Note

Subsection (4)(b) was amended by s.104(2)(a) of the Civil Partnership and Certain Rights and Obligations of Cohabitants Act 2010 (No. 24 of 2010), with effect from 1 January 2011 (S.I. No. 648 of 2010).

Section 5(1) states the kernel of an enduring power, which is that the donor intends it to be effective during his or her subsequent mental incapacity. (See definition of "mental incapacity".)

Subsection (2) empowers the Minister to make regulations in relation to certain matters concerning enduring powers. These regulations have been made and are embodied in S.I. Nos 196 and 287 of 1996 (see Appendices A and B below, pp.47 and 69).

The regulations are quite technical and ought to be followed slavishly by practitioners. Inter alia, they provide for the form and execution of enduring powers. Section 10(5)(a) provides that the enduring power shall be treated as sufficient in point of form and expression if it differs in an immaterial respect from the form prescribed by the regulations. Furthermore, s.10(5)(b) provides that the court may—although the enduring power does not comply with the provisions of s.5 or regulations made thereunder—register the enduring power under certain circumstances. No practitioner will want to run the risk of having to make an application to the court (and presumably pay the costs thereof) because he or she was not careful enough in preparing the enduring power.

In a judgment given by Finnegan P. (as he then was) on 22 March 2002, in *In the matter of the Powers of Attorney Act 1996 and in the matter of an instrument creating an enduring power of attorney executed by Anna (otherwise Nancy) Reid of Seanchara, Community Unit, St. Canice's Road, Finglas, Dublin, 11 on the 11th day of December 1997 and in the matter of an application by Joan Cowan, Terry Reid and Geraldine O'Connor* (unreported, High Court, Finnegan P., 22 March 2002), the judge referred to the refusal of the Registrar of Wards of Court to register an enduring power because the words "I intend this power to be effective during any subsequent mental incapacity of mine", which were contained in the Form prescribed by S.I. No. 196 of 1996, were omitted. The applicants applied to the High Court under s.10(5)(a) and (b) of the Act (see later). The judge did not regard the enduring power as differing in an immaterial respect from the prescribed form, and refused the application on this basis. However, the judge was satisfied on a reading of Part B of the prescribed form in this case that the donor intended the power to be effective during any subsequent mental incapacity, and was further satisfied on oral evidence as to the other matters upon which he was required to be satisfied under s.10(5)(b). He thereupon ordered the enduring power to be registered.

The Law Society of Ireland published very helpful Guidelines: *Enduring Powers of Attorney Guidelines for Solicitors* (see Appendix D).

The Regulations provide for an Explanatory Memorandum, which forms part of the enduring power, to ensure that the latter incorporates adequate information as to the effect of creating or accepting the power.

It is interesting to note at this stage that the power has to be executed by four classes of people: the donor, a solicitor, a registered medical practitioner, and the attorney.

The making of the statement by the registered medical practitioner (that, in his or her opinion, at the time the document was executed the donor had mental capacity) was made slightly easier by the addition in the Act of the words "in his or her opinion" in s.5(2)(d)(iii) (and see *Re W. (Power of Attorney)* [2000] 1 All E.R. 175 (see further, p.21)).

The statement to be made by the attorney (that he or she understands the requirements of registration under s.10) was strengthened by the addition in the Act of the words "the duties and obligations of an attorney".

Subparagraphs (e) and (f) of s.5(2) had not been included in the Bill and were added to the Act to allay concerns that attorneys might not keep adequate accounts or might remunerate themselves in an uncontrolled way. The regulations provide that an attorney "shall keep adequate accounts of the management" of the property and affairs of the donor and "in particular, of any expenditure to meet the needs of persons other than the donor or to make any gifts authorised by the enduring power". The regulations also provide that the enduring power "may make provision in relation to the remuneration of an attorney". If no such provision is made, then the attorney can only recover out of pocket expenses.

The regulations provide that notice of the execution of the enduring power by the donor "shall be given by or on behalf of the donor to at least two persons named by the donor in the enduring power". None of them shall be an attorney under the power. At least one of them shall be:

1. the donor's spouse, if living with the donor; or
2. if clause (i) does not apply, a child of the donor; or
3. if clauses (i) and (ii) do not apply, a relative (if any) of the donor. The form of notice of execution is given in the regulations.

Subsection (3) was not in the Bill and was added to permit the appointment of substitute attorneys to act in the circumstances specified in the subsection.

As originally drafted in the Bill, subs.(4)(a)(i) simply referred to "an individual who has attained 18 years and is not a bankrupt". The additions were made in the interests of protecting a donor against a dishonest or oppressive attorney.

Subsection (4)(b) was supplemented by the substitution for the words "in the employment of" by the words "an employee or agent".

Subsection (6) provides for the invalidation of an enduring power when the circumstances mentioned therein arise, including the bankruptcy, winding up or dissolution of the attorney, or the attorney becoming an owner of a nursing home in which the donor resides.

Subsection (7)(a) was substituted by s.50 of the Family Law (Divorce) Act 1996 (No. 33 of 1996) which came into effect on 27 February 1996.

Subsection (7) was widened, as a result of representations made after the publication of the Bill, by the addition of subparagraphs (c) and (d). Subsection (7) was amended by s.50 of the Family Law (Divorce) Act 1996 by the substitution of the following paragraph:

"(a) The marriage is annulled or dissolved either—
 (i) Under the law of the State, or
 (ii) Under the law of another State and is, by reason of that annulment or divorce, not or no longer a subsisting valid marriage under the law of the State,".

Subsection (8) provides that the enduring power shall not be invalidated by reason of subs.(6) to the extent that it authorises the attorney to make personal care decisions, unless the attorney has been convicted of an offence against the person of the donor or has become disqualified by subs.(4)(b).

Subsection (10) refers to the disclaimer of enduring powers by their attorneys, providing that a disclaimer of an enduring power which has not been registered shall not be effective unless and until the attorney has given notice of disclaimer to the donor. After an enduring power has been registered it can only be disclaimed, on notice to the donor, with the consent of the court.

It should be noted that subs.(11) substantially widens the definition of "owner" of a nursing home.

Scope of authority of attorney under enduring power

6.—(1) An enduring power may confer general authority (as defined in subsection (2)) on the attorney to act on the donor's behalf in relation to all or a specified part of the property and affairs of the donor or may confer on the attorney authority to do specified things on the donor's behalf and the authority may, in either case, be conferred subject to conditions and restrictions.

(2) Where an instrument is expressed to confer general authority on the attorney, it operates to confer, subject to the restriction imposed by subsection (5) and to any conditions or restrictions contained in the instrument, authority to do on behalf of the donor anything which the donor can lawfully do by attorney.

(3) **[** … **]**

(4) Subject to any conditions or restrictions contained in the instrument, an attorney under an enduring power, whether general or limited, may act under the power for the attorney's benefit or that of other persons to the following extent but no further, that is to say, the attorney—

(a) may so act in relation to himself or herself or in relation to any other person if the donor might be expected to provide for his or her or that person's needs respectively; and

(b) may do whatever the donor might be expected to do to meet those needs.

(5) Without prejudice to subsection (4) but subject to any conditions or restrictions contained in the instrument, an attorney under an enduring power, whether general or limited, may, if specific provision to that effect is made in the instrument, dispose of the property of the donor by way of gift to the following extent but no further, that is to say, by making—

(a) gifts of a seasonal nature or at a time, or on an anniversary, of a birth or marriage, to persons (including the attorney) who are related to or connected with the donor, and

(b) gifts to any charity to which the donor made or might be expected to make gifts,

provided that the value of each such gift is not unreasonable having regard to all the circumstances and in particular the extent of the donor's assets.

(6) An enduring power may also confer authority on the attorney to make any specified personal care decision or decisions on the donor's behalf.

(7)(a) Any personal care decision made by an attorney on behalf of a donor shall be made in the donor's best interests.

(b) In deciding what is in a donor's best interests regard shall be had to the following:

(i) so far as ascertainable, the past and present wishes and feelings of the donor and the factors which the donor would consider if he or she were able to do so;

(ii) the need to permit and encourage the donor to participate, or to improve the donor's ability to participate, as fully as possible in any decision affecting the donor;

(iii) so far as it is practicable and appropriate to consult any of the persons mentioned below, their views as to the donor's wishes and feelings and as to what would be in the donor's best interests:

(I) any person named by the donor as someone to be consulted on those matters;

(II) anyone (whether the donor's spouse [or civil partner within the meaning of the Civil Partnership and Certain Rights and Obligations of Cohabitants Act 2010], a relative, friend or other person) engaged in caring for the donor or interested in the donor's welfare;

(iv) whether the purpose for which any decision is required can be as effectively achieved in a manner less restrictive of the donor's freedom of action.

(c) In the case of any personal care decision made by an attorney it shall be a sufficient compliance with paragraph (a) if the attorney reasonably believes that what he or she decides is in the best interests of the donor.

General Note

Section 6(1) provides that the enduring power can confer general authority on the attorney, or authority to do specified things on the donor's behalf. Subsection (2) defines "general authority" in a rather unhelpful way, providing that "general authority" is authority to do anything which the donor could lawfully do by attorney. At common law, an attorney has no power to make gifts (*Re Bowles* (1874) 31 L.T. 365). Nor can an attorney make a will for the donor. However, see subs.(5), which gives the donee the power to make certain gifts in certain circumstances. While the basic rule is that an agent has no right to delegate, having decided on the course of action authorised by the power of attorney, an attorney has authority to employ, e.g. solicitors, auctioneers, accountants and so on, to implement that decision (see *Ex-parte Frampton*; *Re Frampton* (1859) 1 De G. & F.&J. 263, C.A.).

Subsection (3) was repealed by s.8(3) and Sch.2 Pt 5 of the Land Conveyancing Law Reform Act 2009 (No. 27 of 2009) with effect from 1 December 2009 (S.I. No. 356 of 2009).

Section 6(3) specifically empowered an attorney under an enduring power to do whatever the donor could have done as a tenant for life under the Settled Land Act 1882, which was repealed by the Land and Conveyancing Law Reform Act 2009. That Act amends s.6(3) by the deletion of ("... or ... as a tenant for life under the Settled Land Act 1882").

Subsection (4) permits an attorney to act for the attorney's own benefit, or for the benefit of other persons, but only if the donor might be expected to provide for the attorney's or that other person's needs, and may only do whatever the donor might be expected to do to meet those needs. The power given to an attorney under subs.(4) is not, therefore, restricted to situations where the donor owes a family or moral duty to the attorney or the other person in question.

Subsection (5) further empowers the attorney, if the enduring power specifically so provides, to make gifts of the property of the donor of a seasonal nature, or at certain times or anniversaries, to people (including the attorney) who are related to or connected with the donor, and gifts to any charity to which the donor made or might be expected to make gifts. The only restriction here is that the value of each gift is not to be unreasonable having regard to all the circumstances and to the extent of the donor's assets. Once again it should be noted that this subsection is quite wide, and authorises certain gifts not only to relations, but also to people who are "connected with" the donor. Paragraph 5 of the Regulations (S.I. No. 196 of 1996) made under s.5 imposes a duty on the attorney to keep a record of any such gifts. It could be argued that an attorney should have been empowered by the Act to make gifts outside of the restrictions imposed by subs.(5), in the context, for example, of inheritance tax planning. However, it would appear that the subsection as drafted does not go as far as to authorise this.

In his judgment in the case of *Lambert v Lyons* (2 March 2010), Murphy J. discussed the relationship arising from the registration of a power of attorney in the following terms: "The relationship arising from the registration of a power of attorney derives from an instrument voluntarily executed by the donor in accordance with statute (Powers of Attorney Act 1996)". Costello ("The Enduring Problem of Powers of Attorney" (1998) 3(2) C.P.L.J. 35) states as follows:

> "At common law an attorney is in a fiduciary position. He must, thus, not allow himself to do anything in which he has a personal interest which may possibly conflict with the interests of the donor; and from this general rule certain specific applications follow (for example, that the attorney keep the donor's money separate from his own: Henry v. Hammond ([1913] 2 K.B. 515). In principle therefore the attorney could never act so as to benefit himself, but a rigorous application of such a principle could cause obvious hardship particularly where a donor and an attorney are related … ."
> (And see *Re W.*, p.21.)

Subsection (6) was an innovation, not having been included in the original Bill. "Personal care decisions" are defined in s.4. It is possible to make one enduring power conferring on a certain attorney the power to make personal care decisions, and a second enduring power conferring on a different attorney the power to make decisions relating to the "affairs" of the donor.

Subsection (7) provides that the personal care decision must be made in the donor's best interests and states that regard must be had to certain circumstances in deciding what is in the donor's best interests. It further provides that certain people must be consulted in relation to the donor's wishes and feelings, and his or her best interests. However, the last word is clearly given to the attorney by subpara.(c) of subs.(7).

The Act is silent as to whether the donee of an enduring power can continue administering the estate of a deceased person of which the donor, who has lost mental capacity, is personal representative. In England, if the donor of an enduring or ordinary power of attorney is entitled to apply for a grant of probate or letters of administration, his or her attorney can apply for administration for the use and benefit of the donor under r.31(1) of the (English) Non-Contentious Probate Rules 1987 (S.I. No. 2024 of 1987) provided he has authority to do so under the power—a general power gives such authority. The grant may be limited until further representation be granted, or in such other way as the Registrar may direct. (These Rules are presently under review in England.) In this jurisdiction, Ord.79 r.23 of the Rules of the Superior Courts (S.I. No. 15 of 1986) provides:

> "In the case of a person residing out of, or about to leave the jurisdiction of the Court, or who, in the opinion of the Court or the Probate Officer, is suffering from a severe continuing physical disability, administration, or administration with the will annexed, may be granted to his attorney, acting under a power of attorney."

It would appear, by reason of the use of the word "physical", that a Grant of Administration cannot be made to the donee of an enduring power as such. However, r.27 may be of assistance in this connection. It provides:

> "In a case where a person of unsound mind has not a committee appointed by the court, a grant may issue to such person as the Probate Officer may by order assign with the consent of the Registrar of Wards of Court. The application for such order shall be grounded on an affidavit of the applicant showing the amount of his assets, the age and residence of the person of unsound mind and his relationship to the applicant together with an affidavit of a medical practitioner relating to the incapacity of such person."

Subsection 7(b)(iii)(II) was amended by s.104(3) of the Civil Partnership and Certain Rights and Obligations of Cohabitants Act 2010 (No. 24 of 2010), with effect from 1 January 2011 (S.I No. 648 of 2010).

Coming into force and survival of enduring power

7.—(1) Where an individual creates an enduring power of attorney—

(a) subject to subsection (2) and section 9, the power shall not come into force until it has been registered under section 10; and

(b) the power shall not be revoked by the donor's subsequent mental incapacity.

(2) Where the attorney has made an application for registration of the instrument then, until the application has been determined, the attorney may take action under the power—

(a) to maintain the donor or prevent loss to the donor's estate,

(b) to maintain the attorney or other persons in so far as that is permitted under section 6(4), or

(c) to make a personal care decision which cannot reasonably be deferred until the application has been determined.

(3) Where the attorney purports to act as provided by subsection (2) then, in favour of a person who deals with the attorney without knowledge that the attorney is acting otherwise than in accordance with that subsection, the transaction between them shall be as valid as if the attorney were acting in accordance therewith.

[(7A) An enduring power in favour of a civil partner within the meaning of the Civil Partnership and Certain Rights and Obligations of Cohabitants Act 2010 shall, unless the power provides otherwise, be invalidated or, as the case may be, cease to be in force if subsequently-

(a) A decree of nullity or a decree of dissolution of the civil partnership is granted or recognised under the law of the State,

(b) A written agreement to separate is entered into between the civil partners, or

(c) A protection order, interim barring order, barring order or safety order is made against the attorney on the application of the donor, or visa versa.**]**

General Note

Section 7(1) provides that the enduring power shall not come into force until it has been registered, subject to subs.(2) and "section 9". One wonders if the reference to "section 9" here should have been a reference to "section 8", and it was indeed so referred to in the Bill (see below).

Subsection (2) provides that where the attorney has applied for registration he or she may act under the power to do certain important things, including maintaining the donor, preventing loss to the donor's assets, and making personal care decisions which cannot reasonably be deferred. Bona fide third parties who deal with the attorney who is acting under subs.(2) are protected by subs.(3).

Subsection (7A) was inserted by s.104(2)(b) of the Civil Partnership and Certain Rights and Obligations of Cohabitants Act 2010 (No. 24 of 2010), with effect from 1 January 2011 (S.I. No. 648 of 2010).

Functions of court prior to registration

8.—Where the court has reason to believe that the donor of an enduring power may be, or may be becoming, mentally incapable and the court is of the opinion that it is necessary, before the instrument creating the power is registered, to exercise any power with respect to the power of attorney or the attorney appointed to act under it which would become exercisable under section 12 on its registration, the court may on application to it by any interested party exercise that power under this section and may do so whether the attorney has or has not made an application to the court for the registration of the instrument.

General Note

Section 8 permits the court to exercise an enduring power on application to the court by any interested party, where the donor may, or may be becoming, mentally incapable and the court is of the opinion that it is necessary to exercise a power under the enduring power. This may be the case if the attorney has, or even if the attorney has not, applied to the court for the registration of the enduring power. This would, for example, apply to a situation where the donor was becoming mentally incapable but the attorney could not be easily contacted.

Application for registration

9.—(1) If the attorney under an enduring power has reason to believe that the donor is or is becoming mentally incapable, the attorney shall, as soon as practicable, make an application to the court for the registration of the instrument creating the power.

(2) Before making the application the attorney shall comply with the provisions as to notice set out in the First Schedule.

(3) The attorney may, before making the application, refer to the court for its determination any question as to the validity of the power.

(4) A certificate to the effect that the donor is, or is becoming, incapable by reason of a mental condition of managing and administering his or her own property and affairs and purporting to be signed by a registered medical practitioner may be accepted as evidence of the matters contained therein.

(5) Any person who, in an application for registration, makes a statement which he or she knows to be false in a material particular shall be liable—

(a) on conviction on indictment, to imprisonment for a term not exceeding two years or to a fine not exceeding £10,000 [€12,697.38], or both; and

(b) on summary conviction, to imprisonment for a term not exceeding six months or to a fine not exceeding £1,000 [€1,269.74], or both.

(6) Pending the making of other provision by rules of court an application under subsection (1) shall be addressed to the Registrar of Wards of Court.

General Note

Section 9 is vital in that it imposes an obligation on the attorney to apply to the court for the registration of the power once the attorney has reason to believe that the donor is or is becoming mentally incapable. Before making the application, the attorney must give the notice referred to in the First Schedule. Interestingly, s.5 did not empower the Minister to make regulations concerning the form of the certificate to be given by the registered medical practitioner under subs.(4) that the donor is or is becoming incapable by reason of a mental condition of managing and administering his or her own property and affairs. This certificate is clearly indispensable to the application for registration. Subsection (4) did not appear in the Bill as originally drafted.

Subsection (6) provides for the application for registration under subs.(1) to be "addressed to the Registrar of Wards of Court". The original procedure for applying for registration was laid down in a Practice Direction. This procedure was quite complicated, involving, for example, the issue of a Special Summons. The Rules of Court (S.I. No. 66 of 2000), reproduced in Appendix C (p.72) provide for a simpler application for registration to be made to the Registrar of Wards of Court.

Registration

10.—(1) On an application for registration being made in compliance with section 9 the Registrar of Wards of Court shall, unless subsection (2) applies, register the instrument to which the application relates.

(2) If, in the case of an application for registration—

(a) a valid notice of objection to the registration pursuant to subsection (3) from a person to whom an attorney has given notice pursuant to paragraph 2(1) of the First Schedule is received by the court before the expiry of the period of five weeks beginning with the date on which that notice was given,

(b) it appears from the application that there is no one to whom notice has been given under paragraph 2 of that Schedule, or

(c) there is reason to believe that appropriate enquiries might bring to light evidence on which the court could be satisfied that one of the grounds of objection set out in subsection (3) was established,

the court shall neither register the instrument nor refuse the application until it has made or caused to be made such enquiries (if any) as it thinks appropriate in the circumstances of the case.

(3) For the purposes of this Act a notice of objection to the registration of an instrument is valid if the objection is made on one or more of the following grounds, namely—

(a) that the power purported to have been created by the instrument was not valid;

(b) that the power created by the instrument is no longer a valid and subsisting power;

(c) that the donor is not or is not becoming mentally incapable;

(d) that, having regard to all the circumstances, the attorney is unsuitable to be the donor's attorney;

(e) that fraud or undue pressure was used to induce the donor to create the power.

(4) The court may refuse the application on any of the grounds of objection set out in subsection (3).

(5)(a) Where an instrument differs in an immaterial respect in form or mode of expression from the form prescribed by regulations under section 5(2)(a) the instrument shall be treated as sufficient in point of form and expression.

(b) The court may, notwithstanding that an instrument may not comply with the provisions of section 5 or regulations made thereunder, register the instrument as an enduring power if it is satisfied—

(i) that the donor intended the power to be effective during any mental incapacity of the donor,

(ii) that the power was not executed as a result of any fraud or undue pressure,

(iii) that the attorney is suitable to be the donor's attorney, and

(iv) that it is desirable in the interests of justice so to register the instrument.

(6) Where at the time of the application for registration there is in force under the Lunacy Regulation (Ireland) Act, 1871, an order appointing a committee of the estate of the donor but the power created by the instrument has not also been revoked, the court shall make such order as seems to it proper in the

circumstances including, if appropriate, an order revoking the order already made under the said Act.

General Note

Section 10(1) provides that the Registrar of Wards of Court shall register the enduring power unless subs.(2) applies. According to the Courts Service website, 241 enduring powers were registered in 2008.

Subsection (2)(a) applies where a valid notice of objection to the registration of the enduring power has been received from a party to whom notice has been given under para.2(1) of the First Schedule (below). Subsection (2)(b) applies where notice has not been given under para.3 of Pt I of the First Schedule (see below). Subsection (2)(c) applies where the Registrar of Wards of Court has reason to believe that one of the grounds of objection set out in para.3 could be established.

Subsection (2) goes on to state that "the court" (meaning the High Court) shall then neither register the enduring power nor refuse the application for registration until it has made appropriate enquiries. Presumably what is intended is that if the Registrar of Wards of Court believes that subs.(2) applies, he or she will inform a judge of the High Court accordingly, and await a decision of the court as to whether the enduring power should or should not be registered.

Subsection (4) provides that the court may refuse the application for registration of the enduring power on any of the grounds of objection set out in subs.(3).

Morris P., in *Re Hamilton's Application* [1999] 2 I.L.R.M. 509, considered an objection to the registration of an enduring power on the basis that the proposed attorneys were not suitable persons within the meaning of s.10 because of the manner in which, it was alleged, they had mismanaged the donor's affairs to the date of the execution of the enduring power. Morris P. held that the complaints of mismanagement were misdirected because at the time of the matters complained of the donor was capable of, and was managing, her affairs. Thus, even if the criticisms were valid, they were not validly made of and concerning the proposed attorneys (see Law Society of Ireland's *Enduring Powers of Attorney Guidelines for Solicitors*, para.2.4.).

Morris P. also held that the word "unsuitable" as used in s.10 does not pertain to the proposed attorney's skill at managing the donor's property and it would be an improper exercise of the discretion vested in the court to refuse to register the power because the chosen attorney did not possess a high degree of management and business skills. The grounds of objection set out in s.10 are fundamental in nature, and for an objection to succeed, a criticism far more fundamental than mere lack of management skills would have to be established. A criticism made of a proposed attorney, to constitute a ground for refusing to register the power, "must far exceed the corresponding test applied by the courts in applications for the removal of a trustee".

Morris P.'s judgment in Hamilton was followed by Kelly P. in *M.L. v D.W.* (otherwise D.B.) (2016) IEHC 164.

The burden of proof lies on the objector—see the judgment of Baker J. in *Re SCR* (2015) IEHC 308 (followed by Kelly P. in M.L.).

The English case of *In Re W. (Power of Attorney)* [2000] 1 All E.R. 175 is instructive. This case concerned objections to the registration of an enduring power. It was held that the onus of proof is on the objectors to establish that one of the grounds of objection exists. If the objectors fail to do so, the court will order the registration of the enduring power. One of the grounds of objection in this case was the donor's lack of capacity to execute the enduring power. The objectors claimed that the instrument was not valid because the donor did not understand the nature and effect of the enduring power. On appeal it was held that there was no requirement that the evidence positively show the necessary understanding, i.e. the onus of proof was not on the attorney to prove the necessary understanding, rather, the court was bound to register the instrument unless the objectors satisfied the court that the necessary understanding was not there. This coincides with the Law Reform Commission's view, expressed in its Report, that there is a presumption of capacity (Ch.4, "Enduring Powers of Attorney", para.C(2)(a)). In the *Re W.* case, the court was more influenced by the opinion of the general practitioner who saw the donor contemporaneously with the execution of the instrument than by the opinion of an expert given some months after the execution of the power. The Law Society of Ireland's *Enduring Powers of Attorney Guidelines for Solicitors* (Appendix E) recommend that the certificate of the medical practitioner be obtained no later than 30 days following the execution of the instrument.

Another objection raised in the *Re W.* case was the unsuitability of the attorney. It was held that hostility between certain members of the donor's family, including the attorney, was not a ground to make the attorney unsuitable, unless the hostility was at such a level as to interfere with the proper administration of the donor's affairs, or would negatively impact on his assets.

The *Re W.* case also discussed the making of gifts by the attorney. The attorney had made gifts of a sizeable nature to herself and other members of the family out of the donor's estate, arguing that this was essentially just estate planning. The court held that whilst this might be the case, it was inappropriate to do so, without the consent of the court. Section 6(5) of the Act does not envisage gifts of the type referred to in the *Re W.* case.

Subsection (3) provides for valid grounds of objection to the registration of the enduring power. It should be noted that registration cannot take place within five weeks from the date notice has been given pursuant to para.2(1) of the First Schedule. Subsection (5) did not appear in the original Bill and is important because it permits an enduring power to be treated as sufficient "in point of form and expression", even though it differs in an immaterial respect from the form prescribed by regulations. Furthermore, even if the enduring power does not comply with the provisions of s.5, or the regulations made thereunder, the court may still register it if it is satisfied with all of the four requirements specified in subs.(5)(b). (And see *Reid*, p.13.)

The *Reid* case may be useful if an application is being made for the registration of an enduring power prepared in a foreign jurisdiction in compliance with that jurisdiction's legislation, which might not sufficiently comply with the requirements of the 1996 Act.

Subsection (5)(b) has been interpreted to permit the registration of an enduring power executed in accordance with English law provided satisfactory affidavit evidence is available to satisfy the requirements of the subsection.

Subsection (6) provides that where a committee has been appointed under the Lunacy Regulation (Ireland) Act 1871, but the enduring power has not also been revoked, the court may make such order as it deems appropriate, including an order revoking the order already made under the said Act.

Effect and proof of registration

11.—(1) The effect of the registration of an instrument is that—

(a) no revocation of the power by the donor shall be valid unless and until the court confirms the revocation under section 12(3);

(b) no disclaimer of the power shall be valid except on notice to the donor and with the consent of the court;

(c) the donor may not extend or restrict the scope of the authority conferred by the instrument and no consent or instruction given by the donor after registration shall, in the case of a consent, confer any right and, in the case of an instruction, impose or confer any obligation or right on or create any liability of the attorney or other persons having notice of the consent or instruction.

(2) Subsection (1) applies for so long as the instrument is registered whether or not the donor is for the time being mentally capable.

(3) On registration of an enduring power the Registrar of Wards of Court shall supply an attested copy of the enduring power to the donor and any persons who were given notice under paragraph 2 of the First Schedule of the application for registration.

(4) Members of the public may inspect the register free of charge during normal office hours.

(5) A document purporting to be a copy, attested by an officer of the Office of Wards of Court, of an instrument registered under this Act shall be evidence of the contents of the instrument and of the fact that it has been so registered.

(6) Subsection (5) is without prejudice to section 21 (proof by certified copies) and to any other method of proof authorised by law.

General Note

Section 11 set out the effects of the registration of the enduring power:

1. After registration, the power cannot be revoked by the donor without the consent of the court. (Although there is no specific provision as to the form of revocation of a power of attorney in the 1996 Act, it is clear that an enduring power may be revoked prior to registration. It would be prudent for the donor, in such circumstances, to give notice of revocation to the donee, to the parties to whom notice of the execution of the power had been given, and to any financial institutions with which the donor has dealt. (See para.2.10 of the Law Society of Ireland's *Enduring Powers of Attorney Guidelines for Solicitors*—Appendix E.) The English courts apply the principles applicable to the revocation of wills to the revocation of powers of attorney (see *Re Sabatini* (1969) 114 Sol. Jo. 35 (Probate Division).) Donors must have the same degree of capacity when revoking an enduring power as they had when they made it.

   It is frequently the case that the donor has given both an ordinary and an enduring power to the same person. If one is revoked, then clearly the other should be revoked simultaneously.
2. The attorney cannot disclaim the power without the consent of the High Court.
3. The donor may not extend or restrict the authority conferred by the power.

Subsection (2) provides that the effects of registration of the power shall apply only for as long as the enduring power is registered, whether or not the donor is mentally incapable.

Functions of court with respect to registered power

12.—(1) Where an instrument has been registered the court shall, on application to it by the donor, the attorney or any other interested party, as the case may be, have the functions set out in subsections (2) to (6).

(2) The court may—

(a) determine any question as to the meaning or effect of the instrument;

(b) give directions with respect to—

(i) the management or disposal by the attorney of the property and affairs of the donor;

(ii) the rendering of accounts by the attorney and the production of the records kept by the attorney for that purpose;

(iii) the remuneration or expenses of the attorney, whether or not in default of or in accordance with any provision made by the instrument, including directions for the repayment of excessive, or the payment of additional, remuneration;

(iv) a personal care decision made or to be made by the attorney;

(c) require the attorney to furnish information or produce documents or things in his or her possession as attorney;

(d) give any consent or authorisation to act which the attorney would have to obtain from a mentally capable donor;

(e) authorise the attorney to act for the attorney's own benefit or that of other persons than the donor otherwise than in accordance with section 6(4) and (5) (but subject to any conditions or restrictions contained in the instrument);

(f) where appropriate, relieve the attorney wholly or partly from any liability incurred or which may have been incurred on account of a breach of duty as attorney.

(3) On application on notice to the attorney made for the purpose by or on behalf of the donor, the court shall confirm the revocation of the power if satisfied that the donor has done whatever is necessary in law to effect an express revocation of the power and was mentally capable of revoking a power of attorney at the time of the purported revocation.

(4) The court may cancel the registration of an instrument in any of the following circumstances, that is to say—

(a) on confirming the revocation of the power under subsection (3) or consenting to a disclaimer under section 11(1)(b);

(b) on giving a direction revoking the power on exercising any of its powers under the Lunacy Regulation (Ireland) Act, 1871;

(c) on being satisfied that the donor is and is likely to remain mentally capable;

(d) on being satisfied that the power has ceased to be in force by the death or adjudication in bankruptcy of the donor or by virtue of subsection (7) or (9) of section 5 or by the death or mental incapacity of the attorney or by virtue of section 5(6);

(e) on being satisfied that the power was not a valid and subsisting enduring power when registration was effected;

(f) on being satisfied that, having regard to all the circumstances, the attorney is unsuitable to be the donor's attorney;

(g) on being satisfied that fraud or undue pressure was used to induce the donor to create the power; or

(h) for any other good and sufficient reason.

(5) Where the court cancels the registration of an instrument on being satisfied of the matters specified in paragraph (f) or (g) of subsection (4) it shall by order revoke the power created by the instrument.

(6) On the cancellation of the registration of an instrument under subsection (4) (other than paragraph (c)) the instrument shall be delivered up to be cancelled, unless the court otherwise directs.

General Note

Section 12 sets out the functions of the court, after the enduring power has been registered, where application is made to the court by the donor, the attorney, or "any other interested party".

It should be noted that subs.(2)(e) permits a court to extend the provisions of s.6(4) and (5), which apply to provision for the needs of the attorney or any other person the donor might be expected to provide for, and certain types of gifts.

Subsection (3) empowers the court to confirm the revocation of the enduring power on the application of the donor in a situation where the donor is mentally capable of revoking the power.

Subsection (4) sets out the court's powers to cancel the registration of an enduring power.

These powers are wide and include the power to cancel the registration of an enduring power "for any other good and sufficient reason". Subsection (4)(h) did not appear in the original Bill.

Subsection (5) provides that where the court cancels the registration of the power on the grounds of the unsuitability of the attorney or for fraud or undue pressure, the court shall also revoke the enduring power.

Subsection (6) provides that when the registration of the enduring power is cancelled, the instrument creating the enduring power shall be delivered up to be cancelled, except in the circumstances where the donor is, and is likely to remain, mentally capable. There is an implication here that if the donor became mentally incapable again, an enduring power could be re-registered.

Protection of attorney and third person where registered power invalid or not in force

13.—(1) Subsections (2) and (3) apply where an instrument which did not create a valid enduring power has been registered, whether or not the registration has been cancelled at the time of the act or transaction in question.

(2) An attorney who acts in pursuance of an enduring power which is not or no longer a valid power or which has ceased to be in force shall not thereby incur any liability (either to the donor or to any other person) unless at the time of acting the attorney knows—

- (a) that the instrument did not create a valid enduring power; or
- (b) that an event has occurred which, if the instrument had recreated a valid enduring power, would have invalidated the power or caused it to cease to be in force; or
- (c) that the instrument has been cancelled.

(3) Any transaction between the attorney and another person shall, in favour of that person, be as valid as if the power had then been in existence, unless at the time of the transaction that person has knowledge of any of the matters mentioned in subsection (2).

(4) Where the interest of a purchaser depends on whether a transaction between the attorney and another person was valid by virtue of subsection (3), it shall be presumed in favour of the purchaser unless the contrary is shown that the transaction was valid if—

- (a) the transaction between that person and the attorney was completed within twelve months of the date on which the instrument was registered; or
- (b) that person makes a statutory declaration, before or within three months after the completion of the purchase, that he or she had no reason at the time of the transaction to doubt that the attorney had authority to dispose of the property which was the subject of the transaction.

(5) For the purposes of section 18 (protection of attorney and third persons where action is taken under the power of attorney in ignorance of its having been revoked) in its application to an enduring power the revocation of which by the donor is by virtue of section 11(1)(a) invalid unless and until confirmed by the court under section 12(3), knowledge of the confirmation of the revocation is, but knowledge of the unconfirmed revocation is not, knowledge of the revocation of the power.

(6) In this section "purchaser" has the meaning assigned to it by section 18(6) and "purchase" shall be construed accordingly.

General Note

Section 13(2) and (3) protect attorneys and third persons who have acted in reliance on the validity of an enduring power, unless they knew: the instrument did not create a valid enduring power; that an event has occurred which would have caused the power to cease to be in force; or that the instrument creating the power has been cancelled. The question arises as to whether those relying on the protection of subss.(2) and (3) should check with the register of enduring powers of attorney kept and maintained by the Registrar of Wards of Court under Ord.129 of the Rules of the Superior Courts (see Appendix C), or can they rely on s.11(5), which provides that a document purporting to be a copy, attested by an officer of the Office of Wards of Court, of an instrument registered under the Act, shall be evidence of the contents of the instrument and of the fact that it has been so registered?

While s.12(6) provides that when an instrument creating a power is cancelled, the instrument shall be delivered up to be cancelled, what if an official copy is still in existence after the cancellation of the instrument? It would, presumably, always be prudent practice to check the Register of Enduring Powers of Attorney.

Subsection (4) provides that it shall be presumed in favour of a purchaser whose interest depends on whether a transaction between the attorney and another person is valid by virtue of subs.(3) that the transaction was valid:

- if the transaction between that person and the attorney was completed within 12 months of the date of registration of the enduring power, or
- if that person makes the statutory declaration referred to in subs.(4)(b).

"Purchaser" is defined in s.18(6). The purchaser must be in good faith and must acquire an interest in property for valuable consideration. Thus, the person who deals directly with the attorney is protected by s.13(3), and the purchaser who deals with that person is protected by s.13(4), provided the provisions of subparas (a) and (b) of subs.(4) are complied with. A duty is here imposed on conveyancers to ensure compliance with subs.(4) where they are acting for someone acquiring property from an attorney, as otherwise they may have difficulties when that person is disposing of the property later.

Subsection (5) helpfully provides that knowledge of the confirmation of the revocation of an enduring power is not knowledge for the purposes of s.18 (see below, p.30) unless the revocation of the power has been confirmed by the court.

It would seem that the register kept and maintained by the Registrar of Wards of Court will continue in being for enduring powers created under the 1996 Act, but it should be noted that under s.72 of the 2015 Act, another register (of enduring powers created under the 2015 Act) shall be established and maintained by the Director of Decision Support Service (as defined in s.94 of the 2015 Act).

The protection afforded to attorneys and third persons by s.13 would not seem to apply to attorneys and third persons who have acted in reliance of an enduring power created under the 2015 Act, because the 1996 Act does not apply to enduring powers created after the commencement date of the 2015 Act (s.81(2)(b) of the 2015 Act). Section 66(8) of the 2015 Act (see p.118) makes provision that a person who relies on a relevant decision made by an attorney under an enduring power who has become disqualified is not precluded from recovering damages in respect of any loss incurred by him or her as a result of that reliance. The presumption in favour of a purchaser of property mentioned in s.13(4) does not seem to apply to purchasers from attorneys appointed under the 2015 Act because of the provisions of s.81(2)(b) of the 2015 Act.

Application to joint and joint and several attorneys

14.—(1) An instrument which appoints more than one person to be an attorney may specify that the attorneys are appointed to act either jointly or jointly and severally. In default, the attorneys shall be deemed to have been appointed to act jointly.

(2) This Act, in its application to joint attorneys, applies to them collectively as it applies to a single attorney but subject to the modifications specified in subsection (3) and Part I of the Second Schedule.

(3) Where two or more persons are appointed (or are deemed to have been appointed) to act jointly, then, in the case of the death, incapacity or disqualification of any one or more of them, the remaining attorney or attorneys may continue to act, whether solely or jointly as the case may be, unless the instrument creating the power expressly provides to the contrary.

(4) This Act, in its application to joint and several attorneys, applies with the modifications specified in subsections (5) to (8) and in Part II of the Second Schedule.

(5) A failure, as respects any other attorney, to comply with the provisions of section 5 and regulations made thereunder shall prevent the instrument from applying in that attorney's case without however affecting its efficacy as respects the other or others.

(6) Where one or more but not both or all the attorneys makes or joins in making an application for registration of the instrument then—

- (a) an attorney who is not an applicant as well as one who is may act pending the determination of the application as provided in section 7(2) (or under section 8);
- (b) notice of the application shall also be given under the First Schedule to the other attorney or attorneys; and
- (c) objection may validly be taken to the registration on a ground relating to an attorney or to the power of an attorney who is not an applicant as well as to one or the power of one who is an applicant.

(7) The court shall not refuse under section 10(4) to register an instrument because a ground of objection to an attorney or a power is established if an enduring power subsists as respects an attorney who is not affected thereby but shall give effect to it by the prescribed qualification of the registration.

(8) The court shall not cancel the registration of an instrument under section 12(4) in any of the circumstances specified in that subsection if an enduring power subsists as respects an attorney who is not affected thereby but shall give effect to it by the prescribed qualification of the registration.

(9) In this section—

"prescribed" means prescribed by rules of court; and

"the requirements for the creation of enduring powers" means the provisions of section 5 other than subsections (5) to (10) and of regulations under subsection (2) of that section.

General Note

In the First Schedule to the Enduring Powers of Attorney Regulations 1996 (S.I. No. 196 of 1996), "Part A: Explanatory Memorandum", it is stated that where the attorneys are appointed jointly, they must all act together and cannot act separately; but when they are appointed jointly and severally, they can all act together, but they can also act separately if they wish. If the enduring power does not specify how the attorneys are to act, they shall be deemed to have been appointed to act jointly. If they are appointed or deemed to have been appointed to act jointly, then under s.14(3), where one of them dies, the remaining attorney or attorneys may continue to act, unless the instrument creating the power expressly provides to the contrary.

Subsection (5) makes it clear that where attorneys are appointed jointly and severally, the failure of one of the attorneys to comply with s.5 of the Act and regulations made thereunder shall not affect the efficacy of the power as respects the other attorney or attorneys. This would not be the case where the appointment was a joint one, because in that circumstance the attorneys must act together and, clearly, if one was failing to comply with s.5 or the regulations, the other or others could not act validly.

Subsection (6) refers to a situation where one or more, but not both or all, of attorneys who are appointed jointly and severally applies for the registration of the instrument creating the power.

Subsection (7) deals with the situation where a ground of objection is established to an attorney, or a power, if the enduring power subsists as regards an attorney who is not thereby affected. Thus, a power could be registered to the exclusion of one or more joint and several attorneys, if no objection is established to a surviving attorney or attorneys. Subsection (8) applies similar considerations to applications for the cancellation of a power.

Part III

Powers of Attorney Generally

General Note

This Part of the Act deals with powers of attorney generally, and some of its provisions would therefore also apply to enduring powers. The law concerning powers of attorney generally, until the passing of the Powers of Attorney Act 1996, was embodied in the common law and in certain provisions of the Conveyancing Acts 1881 and 1882. Some provisions of these Acts are repealed by the Powers of Attorney Act 1996 (see General Note to s.25 below, p.37).

Creation of power

15.—(1) Where an instrument creating a power of attorney is signed by direction of the donor it shall be signed in the presence of the donor and of another person who shall attest the instrument as witness.

(2) A power of attorney is not required to be made under seal.

(3) This section is without prejudice to any requirement in or under any other enactment as to the witnessing of powers of attorney or as to the execution of instruments by bodies corporate.

General Note

Section 15(1) refers to an instrument creating a power of attorney being signed by direction of the donor, presumably in circumstances where the donor is physically (but obviously not mentally) incapable of signing. Subsection (2) dispenses with the requirement that a power of attorney should be under seal (see General Note to s.2, above, p.8). Subsection (3) contains a saver for any other statutory requirements for witnessing powers of attorney and for the rules governing the execution of instruments by bodies corporate.

Effect of general power in specified form

16.—(1) A general power of attorney in the form set out in the Third Schedule, or in a form to the like effect expressed to be made under this Act, shall operate to confer on the donee or donees of the power acting in accordance with its terms authority to do on behalf of the donor anything which the donor can lawfully do by attorney.

(2) This section does not apply to functions which the donor has as a trustee or personal representative **[** ... **]**.

General Note

Section 16 provides for the creation of a form (set out in the Third Schedule, p.45) of general power of attorney, which operates in the widest fashion, empowering the donee to do anything that the donor could lawfully do by attorney. The form gives practitioners the option of offering their clients a very simple form of general power of attorney.

Subsection (2) was amended by s.8(1) and Sch.1 of the Land Conveyancing Law Reform Act 2009 (No. 27 of 2009), with effect from 1 December 2009 (S.I. No. 356 of 2009), by the deletion of "or as a tenant for life within the meaning of the Settled Land Act, 1882, or as a trustee or other person exercising the power of a tenant for life under section 60 of that Act".

Execution of instruments, etc. by donee of power

17.—(1) The donee of a power of attorney may—

(a) execute any instrument with his or her own signature and, where sealing is required, with his or her own seal, and

(b) do any other thing in his or her own name,

by the authority of the donor of the power; and any instrument executed or thing done in that manner shall be as effective as if executed or done by the donee with the signature and seal, or, as the case may be, in the name, of the donor of the power.

(2) A person who is authorised under a power of attorney to convey any estate or interest in property in the name or on behalf of a corporation sole or aggregate may either execute the conveyance as provided in subsection (1) or, as donee of the power, execute the conveyance by signing his or her name as acting in the name or on behalf of the corporation in the presence of at least one witness and, in the case of a deed, by affixing his or her own seal, and such execution takes effect and is valid in like manner as if the corporation had executed the conveyance.

(3) Where a corporation aggregate is authorised under a power of attorney to convey any interest in property in the name or on behalf of any other person (including another body corporate), a person appointed for that purpose by the corporation may execute the deed or other instrument in the name of such other person; and where an instrument appears to be executed by a person so appointed then in favour of a purchaser the instrument is deemed to have been executed by that person, unless the contrary is shown.

(4) In this section "purchaser" has the meaning given to it by section 18(6).

(5) This section applies whenever the power of attorney was created.

General Note

Section 17(1) re-enacts s.46 of the Conveyancing Act 1881, which authorised a donee of power to execute or do any assurance, instrument or thing in and with his or her own name, signature and seal (where sealing is required) by the authority of the donor. Section 46 of the Conveyancing Act 1881 related solely to the execution of deeds by an attorney. Section 17(1) of the 1996 Act provides that the donee of a power of attorney may execute any instrument or do any other thing either in his or her own name (with his or her own signature or seal where appropriate) and by the authority of the donor, or in the name of the donor. Where a company is acting as attorney, any individual appointed for that purpose by the company may execute a deed or other instrument in the name of the donor. Such execution will be valid in favour of a purchaser where the instrument indicated that the person executing it had such authority, unless the contrary is shown.

Section 17(2) provides that were a power of attorney is being exercised on behalf of a corporation, the donee may execute a conveyance "by signing his or her own name as acting in the name or on behalf of the corporation in the presence of at least one witness and, in the case of a deed, by affixing his or her own seal". Although the general provision in subs. (1) applies, it would be prudent for this special method of execution to be used whenever a conveyance of property is made by an attorney on behalf of a corporation.

The best practice in relation to the execution of deeds by the donee of a power of attorney is as follows:

1. The deed is prepared in the name of the donor;
2. The attestation clause states that the deed is executed on behalf of the donor by the attorney;
3. The donee executes by writing in his or her own hand, "AB (the donor) by his or her attorney CD (the donee)", who then signs his or her own name.

Subsection (3) authorises bodies aggregate, when donees of powers of attorney, to appoint persons to execute a deed to convey any interest in property in the name of the donor of a power. Subsection (4) gives the meaning to "purchaser" that is given by s.18(6).

Subsection (5) applies s.17 to powers of attorney executed either before or after the coming into operation of the Powers of Attorney Act 1996. Presumably, this subsection therefore corrects any invalidity in the execution by a donee of a power in the sense that a form of execution, which may have been invalid prior to 1 August 1996, may be valid thereafter.

Protection of donee and other persons where power revoked

18.—(1) A donee of a power of attorney who acts in pursuance of the power at a time when it has been revoked shall not, by reason of the revocation, incur any liability (either to the donor or to any other person) if at that time the donee did not know that the power had been revoked.

(2) Where a power of attorney has been revoked and a person, without knowledge of the revocation, deals with the donee of the power, the transaction between them shall, in favour of that person, be as valid as if the power had then been in force.

(3) Where the power is expressed in the instrument creating it to be irrevocable and to be given by way of security then, unless the person dealing with the donee knows that it was not in fact given by way of security, that person shall be entitled to assume that the power is incapable of revocation except by the donor acting with the consent of the donee and shall accordingly be treated for the purposes of subsection (2) as having knowledge of the revocation only if that person knows that it has been revoked in that manner.

(4) Where the interest of a purchaser depends on whether a transaction between the donee of a power of attorney and another person was valid by virtue of subsection (2), it shall be presumed in favour of the purchaser unless the contrary is shown that that person did not at the material time know of the revocation of the power if—

(a) the transaction between that person and the donee was completed within twelve months of the date on which the power came into operation, or

(b) that person makes a statutory declaration, before or within three months after the completion of the purchase, that that person did not at the material time know of the revocation of the power.

(5) Without prejudice to subsection (3), for the purposes of this section

knowledge of the revocation of a power of attorney includes knowledge of the occurrence of any event (such as the death of the donor) which has the effect of revoking the power.

(6) In this section "purchaser" means a purchaser in good faith for valuable consideration and includes a lessee, mortgagee or other person who, for valuable consideration, acquires an interest in any property; and includes also an intending purchaser.

(7) This section applies to a power of attorney whenever created but only to acts and transactions after the commencement of this section.

General Note

Section 18 applies both to enduring powers and to ordinary powers of attorney, but in its application to enduring powers, practitioners should refer back to s.13(5). Section 18 replaces ss.8 and 9 of the Conveyancing Act 1882 and relates to the protection of the donee of a power of attorney and third parties where the power is revoked. The protection given by s.18 to donees of enduring powers and other persons dealing with such donees does not appear to apply to donees appointed under the provisions of the 2015 Act, because of the provisions of s.81(2)(b) of that Act—see p.136.

Section 8(1) of the Conveyancing Act 1882 provided:

> "If a power of attorney, given for valuable consideration, is in the instrument creating the power expressed to be irrevocable, then, in favour of a purchaser,—
>
> (i) The power shall not be revoked at any time, either by anything done by the donor of the power without the concurrence of the donee of the power, or by the death, marriage, lunacy, unsoundness of mind or bankruptcy of the donor of the power; and
>
> (ii) Any Act done at any time by the donee of the power, in pursuance of the power, shall be as valid as if anything done by the donor of the power without the concurrence of the donee of the power, or the death, marriage, lunacy, unsoundness of mind, or bankruptcy of the donor of the power had not been done or happened; and
>
> (iii) Neither the donee of the power nor the purchaser shall at any time be prejudicially affected by notice of anything done by the donor of the power without he concurrence of the donee of the power, or of the death, marriage, lunacy, unsoundness of mind or bankruptcy of the donor of the power.
>
> (2) This section applies only to powers of attorney created by instruments executed after the commencement of this Act."

Section 8 of the 1882 Act applied only to powers of attorney given for valuable consideration, which are expressed in the instrument creating the power to be irrevocable (see Wylie, *Irish Land Law*, 5th edn (Haywards Heath, West Sussex: Bloomsbury, 2013), paras 11.37 to 11.43).

Section 9 of the Conveyancing Act 1882 provided:

> "(1) If a power of attorney, whether given for valuable consideration or not, is in the instrument creating the power expressed to be irrevocable for a fixed time therein specified, not exceeding one year from the date of the instrument, then, in favour of a purchaser,—
>
> (i) The power shall not be revoked, for and during that fixed time, either by anything done by the donor of the power without the concurrence of the donee of the power, or by the death, marriage, lunacy, unsoundness of mind or bankruptcy of the donor of the power; and
>
> (ii) Any act donees in that fixed time, the donee of the power, in pursuance of the power, shall be as valid as if anything done by the donor of the power without the concurrence of the donee of the power, or the death, marriage, lunacy, unsoundness of mind, or bankruptcy of the donor that the power had not been done or happened; and
>
> (iii) Neither the donee of the power, nor the purchaser, shall at any time

prejudicially affected by notice either during or after that fixed time of anything done by the donor of the power during that fixed time, without the concurrence of the donee of the power, or of the death, marriage, lunacy, unsoundness of mind, or bankruptcy of the donor of the power within that fixed time.

(2) This section applies only to powers of attorney created by instruments executed after the commencement of this Act."

The protection afforded by these sections to donees and purchasers where the power of attorney has been revoked was removed by the 1996 Act and replaced by the protection given by s.18 of that Act.

It should be noted, of course, that an enduring power cannot be revoked after registration without the confirmation of the court (see s.12(3) and (4)(a)). An enduring power may be revoked prior to registration, but this revocation can be of no significance to donees or purchasers, because enduring power cannot come into force until it has been registered under s.10.

Section 7(2) of the 1996 Act does empower an attorney who has made an application for registration, until the application has been determined, to take action to, inter alia, maintain the donor or prevent loss to the donor's estate. Section 7(3) protects a person who deals with the attorney "without knowledge that the attorney is acting otherwise than in accordance with that subsection" where the attorney purports to act as provided by s.7(2). The transaction between the attorney and such person shall be as valid as if the attorney were acting in accordance with s.7(2).

At common law, a power of attorney was a "revokable instrument" (see *Bromley v Holland* (1802) 7 Ves. 3), and so the donor can revoke at any time unless it is an irrevocable power. It appears that the revocation can be oral, in writing or by deed (see *Re "The Margaret Mitchell"* (1888 Swab 382, 166 E.R. 174), but it is ineffective until it is received by the donee (see *Re Oriental Bank Corporation, ex-parte Guillemin* (1884) 28 Ch. D. 634). It appears that notice to one joint attorney is effective (see *Bristow and Porter v Taylor* (1817) 2 Stark 50, 171 E.R. 568).

There would be no benefit in making an enduring power irrevocable, because an application can always be made to the court, after registration, to confirm revocation, and the enduring power cannot be used prior to registration except in the limited context of s.7.

Prior to the implementation of the 1996 Act, in relation to an ordinary power that is expressed to be irrevocable, donees and purchasers only had protection where the period of irrevocability did not exceed one year (see s.9 of the Conveyancing Act 1882, as quoted above). Apart from the case of the power given on security (see s.20, below, p.33) there is now no benefit in making an ordinary power irrevocable, as the protection given by s.18 to donees and persons dealing with the donee applies whether or not the power is expressed to be irrevocable.

Section 18(1) deals with the protection of a donee who acts in pursuance of a power at a time when it has been revoked, if he or she did not know at that time that it had been revoked. In such circumstances, the donee does not incur any liability either to the donor or to any other person.

Subsection (2) confers protection on a third party who deals with a donee of a power which has been revoked without that third party's knowledge of the revocation. It is, therefore, essential that notice that the power has been revoked should be given to anyone who might rely on it.

Subsection (3) refers to powers which are expressed to be irrevocable and given by way of security (see s.20, below, p.33).

Subsection (4) is similar to s.13(4), with some differences. Section 13 deals with the protection of attorneys and third persons where a registered enduring power is invalid and not in force, while s.18 deals with the protection of donees and other persons where a power has been revoked. The protection given by s.18 to third parties must be qualified in respect of enduring powers by the fact that their revocation becomes valid when confirmed by the court. Thus, a person relying on an enduring power should check the register to ensure that the registration of the enduring power has not been revoked. The provisions of s.13(5) are relevant here.

The presumption in s.18(4) is that the purchaser "did not at the material time know of the revocation of the power" whereas the presumption in s.13(4) is "that the transaction was valid". Subparagraph (b) in s.18(4) provides that the statutory declaration must state that the purchaser "did not at the material time know of the revocation of the power", whereas subparagraph (b) of s.13(4) provides that the declaration must state that that person "had no reason at the time of transaction to doubt that the attorney had authority to dispose of the property which was the subject of the transaction".

Subsection (5) gives further protection to a person dealing with the donee of a power without knowledge of the occurrence of any event which has the effect of revoking the power.

Subsection (6) contains the definition of "purchaser" which is similar to the definition of "purchaser" in the Conveyancing Acts, but "includes also an intending purchaser". The subsection (6) definition of purchaser includes the ingredient of "good faith" which does not appear in the definition of purchaser in s.1 of the Conveyancing Act 1882. Presumably, the presumption contained in s.18(4) overrides any constructive notice which a purchaser might be deemed to have under s.3 of the Conveyancing Act 1882 (see Wylie, *Irish Land Law*, 5th edn (Haywards Heath, West Sussex: Bloomsbury, 2013), paras 3.89 and following).

Subsection (7) applies s.18 to powers of attorney whenever created, but only to acts and transactions after the commencement of that section. Note, however, the amended definition of "purchaser" in s.3 of the Land and Conveyancing Law Reform Act 2009. This amendment does not appear to apply to s.18(6).

Protection of transferee under stock exchange transaction

19.—(1) Without prejudice to section 18, where—

(a) the donee of a power of attorney executes, as transferor, an instrument transferring registered securities, and

(b) the instrument is executed for the purposes of a stock exchange transaction,

it shall be presumed in favour of the transferee unless the contrary is shown that the power had not been revoked at the date of the instrument if a statutory declaration to that effect is made by the donee of the power on or within three months after that date.

(2) In this section "registered securities" and "stock exchange transaction" have the same meanings as in the Stock Transfer Act, 1963.

General Note

Section 19 applies to enduring powers and to ordinary powers of attorney. It confers special protection on the transferee of registered securities which are transferred by the donee of a power of attorney for the purposes of a stock exchange transaction. The section creates a presumption in favour of such a transferee (unless the contrary is shown) that the power had not been revoked at the date of the instrument, if a statutory declaration to that effect is made by the donee of the power on or within three months after that date. "Registered securities" and "stock exchange transactions" have the same meanings as in the Stock Transfer Act 1963. This section mirrors s.6(1) of the UK Powers of Attorney Act 1971, except in one important respect. In the UK section the presumption is "conclusive" while in the Irish section the presumption is "unless the contrary is shown".

Power given as security

20.—(1) Where a power of attorney is expressed to be irrevocable and is given to secure—

(a) a proprietary interest of the donee of the power, or

(b) the performance of an obligation owed to the donee,

then, so long as the donee has that interest or the obligation remains undischarged, the power shall not be revoked—

(i) by the donor without the consent of the donee, or

(ii) by the death, incapacity or bankruptcy of the donor or, if the donor is a body corporate, by its winding-up or dissolution.

(2) A power of attorney given to secure a proprietary interest may be given, and shall be deemed to have been capable always of being given, to the person entitled to the interest and persons deriving title under that person to that interest, and those persons shall be duly constituted donees of the power for all purposes of the power but without prejudice to any right to appoint substitutes given by the power.

[(3) This section does not apply to a power of attorney that was given otherwise than to secure an interest, or the performance of an obligation, referred to in subsection (1) and was created by an instrument executed before the 1st day of August 1996 but, subject to the foregoing, applies to powers of attorney whenever created.]

General Note

Section 20 confirms the law relating to powers of attorney given for security, where the power of attorney is expressed to be irrevocable and is given to secure a proprietary interest of the donee of the power, or the performance of an obligation owed to the donee. So long as the donee has that interest, or the obligation remains undischarged, power shall not be revoked:

1. By the donor, without the consent of the donee; or
2. By the death, incapacity or bankruptcy of the donor, or if the donor is a body corporate, by its winding up or dissolution.

Subsection (2) provides a power of attorney given to secure a proprietary interest will run with the ownership of that interest and the person entitled to the interest; and persons still having title under that person to that interest, which shall be duly constituted donees of the power for all purposes of the power, but without prejudice to any right to appoint substitutes given by the power. This section applies to powers of attorney whenever created. It is unlikely that this section can apply to enduring powers because they cannot be "expressed to be irrevocable". The statutory instrument providing for the form of enduring powers does not envisage such a provision.

Section 5 of the Family Law (Miscellaneous Provisions) Act 1997 amended s.20 of the 1996 Act, by the substitution of the following subsection for subs.(3).

Subsection (3) was substituted by s.5 of the Family Law (Miscellaneous Provisions) Act 1997 (No. 18 of 1997), which came into effect on 5 May 1997.

This amendment is obscure and the Explanatory Memorandum does not appear to throw any light on it. It ensures, certainly, that irrevocable powers of attorney given prior to the enactment of the Powers of Attorney Act 1996, otherwise than to secure an interest, or performance of an obligation, are not affected by s.20. Reasons for the amendment of subs. (3) were given by the Minister of State at the Department of Enterprise and Employment (see 478 *Dáil Debates* Cols 325–326 (second stage)). The Minister stated:

> "Section 20 of the 1996 Act made it clear the only powers which ought to be irrevocable should be those given by way of security, for example, to protect a mortgagee in the event of default in repayments by the Donor of the Power. This Section applies to Powers of Attorney whenever created. When the 1996 Act was introduced, it was widely understood there were no cases where Powers of Attorney had been granted otherwise than by way of security. However the attention of the Minister for Equality and Law Reform has recently been drawn to a case where a person had given a Power of Attorney which was expressed to be irrevocable and was in consideration of an annual payment to the donees. The intention of the donor was that the donees should be in a position to act in the event of the donor's incapacity. Legal advice was obtained by the parties to the effect that the power was valid under section 8 of the 1882 Act [the Conveyancing Act 1882]. Although there may be other similar cases none have so

far been reported. The Minister for Equality and Law Reform is of the view that any power of attorney given before the date on which the 1996 Act came into operation under the 1882 Act, otherwise than by way of security, should not be so affected by section 20 of the 1996 Act. Accordingly he has provided in section 5 that section 20 shall not invalidate powers of attorney given otherwise than by way of security under sections 8 and 9 of the 1882 Act."

Proof of instrument creating power

21.—(1) A power of attorney may be proved by production of the original instrument or of a copy which—

(a) is certified by the donor of the power or by a solicitor or member firm (within the meaning of the Stock Exchange Act, 1995), or in such other manner as the court approves, to be a true copy of the original, or

(b) where the instrument has been deposited in the Central Office of the High Court pursuant to section 22 is attested in accordance with that section.

(2) It is immaterial for the purposes of subsection (1) how many removes there are between the copy and the original or by what means (which may include facsimile transmission) the copy produced or any intermediate copy was made.

(3) This section is without prejudice to any other method of proof authorised by law.

General Note

Section 21 introduces a new method of proving powers of attorney. Although this section is not excluded from applying to enduring powers, it would seem prudent to rely on s.11(5) in relation to the proof of the contents of an enduring power and the fact that it has been registered. Heretofore one had to rely on s.48(4) of the Conveyancing Act 1881 to prove the contents of a power of attorney. Section 48 is repealed by the Powers of Attorney Act 1996. Section 48(4) of the 1881 Act provided that:

> "An office copy of an instrument so deposited shall without further proof be sufficient evidence of the contents of the instrument and of the deposit thereof in the Central Office".

Thus, in order to prove a power of attorney prior to the 1996 Act, one had to produce either the original or a Central Office certified copy thereof. In Land Registry dealings, the original power of attorney, or the Central Office certified copy, had to be lodged in the Land Registry and a solicitor's certified copy would not suffice. Rule 55 of the Land Registry Rules 1972 provided as follows:

> "(1) Where an application or instrument is executed by attorney, the power of attorney, or an office copy thereof, shall be produced to the Authority; and, in cases not within sections 8 and 9 of the Conveyancing Act 1882, evidence shall also be given that the principal was alive at the time of the execution of the instrument and that the power was then unrevoked.
>
> (2) The power of attorney or an office copy thereof shall be filed in the Registry."

This was amended consequent upon the enactment of the Powers of Attorney Act 1996. Rule 55 of the Land Registration Rules 2012 (the "2012 Rules") provides as follows:

> "55. Where an application or instrument is executed by attorney, the Power of Attorney, or a certified copy made pursuant to section 21 of the Powers of Attorney Act 1996, or an attested copy made pursuant to section 22 of that Act shall be produced to the Authority."

The Land Registry Legal Office Notice 3/2010 (updated 1 February 2013) explains the provisions of the 1996 Act and refers to r.55 of the 2012 Rules. However, it goes on to state in para.8 thereof, under the heading of "Protection against Fraud":

"There have been numerous instances in other jurisdictions, with similar title registration regimes, of fraudulent transfers and charges involving the use of forged powers of attorney. Henceforth it will be a requirement that a power of attorney be accompanied by a legal statement from the solicitor for the donee that they have reviewed and discussed the original signed and witnessed power with their client donee, and the clients have confirmed that they are the lawful party named in the document, that it is still in force and that they are acting within the scope of the power granted."

Section 21 provides that a power of attorney may be proved by the production of the original instrument or of a copy certified by the donor, or by a solicitor, or by a member firm (within the meaning of the Stock Exchange Act 1995), or in such other manner as the court approves. Alternatively, where the instrument has been deposited in the Central Office in the High Court, pursuant to s.22 of the 1996 Act, it may be proved by a copy attested in accordance with that section. Convenience would therefore appear to dictate that a power of attorney should not be deposited in the Central Office, because in such circumstances a copy thereof certified in accordance with s.21(1)(a) will not suffice.

Section 21(2) further facilitates proof of a power of attorney, by providing that it is immaterial how many removes there are between the copy and the original, or by what means the copy was produced, or any intermediate copy thereof was made. Subsection (2) can presumably only apply to powers of attorney which have not been deposited in the Central Office.

It is not provided that this section applies to powers of attorney whenever executed. In the light of the provision of s.22(6), it must be assumed that s.21 only applies to powers of attorney created after the 1996 Act came into operation.

Deposit of original instruments in Central Office

22.—(1) An instrument creating a power of attorney, its execution being verified by affidavit, statutory declaration or other sufficient evidence, may, with the affidavit or declaration, if any, be deposited in the Central Office of the High Court.

(2) A separate file of instruments so deposited shall be kept and any person may, free of charge during normal office hours, search that file and inspect any instrument so deposited, and an attested copy thereof shall be delivered to that person on request.

(3) A copy of an instrument so deposited may be presented at the Central Office, and may be stamped or marked as an attested copy, and when so stamped or marked shall become and be an attested copy.

(4) An attested copy of an instrument so deposited shall without further proof be sufficient evidence of the contents of the instrument and of the deposit thereof in the Central Office.

(5) Subsections (2) to (4) apply to instruments deposited in the Central Office before the commencement of this section.

(6) This section applies to instruments creating powers of attorney whenever executed.

General Note

Section 22 mirrors s.48 of the Conveyancing Act 1881 (see above). Subsection (5) was added after the Committee Stage of the Bill had been concluded by the Select Committee on Legislation and Security. It is difficult to understand why subs.(5) is necessary, having regard to subs.(6).

It is understood that representations were made by the Law Society Conveyancing Committee to the Minister to drop s.22 entirely, or make it mandatory. Many feel that s.22 creates confusion, with some practitioners insisting that all powers of attorney be deposited in the Central Office, while others point to the fact that s.22 is not mandatory. In practice, some solicitors have insisted that powers of attorney be deposited in the Central Office, notwithstanding the fact that this does not add to the validity of the power in any way. It could be said that the only advantage to depositing a power of attorney in the Central Office is that if the power of attorney is lost, an attested copy can be obtained. It is, however, clear that s.22 is not mandatory and that powers of attorney do not have to be deposited in the Central Office to be valid. Order 78 of the Rules of the Superior Courts provides for the deposit of Powers of Attorney in the Central Office.

At common law, the certified copy is not proof of the truth of the contents or as to the genuineness of the execution of the document creating the power (see *O'Kane v Mullan* (1925) N.I. 1 and *Re Airey* (1897) 1 Ch. 164). Note that while s.22 refers to the proof of the contents of the power of attorney, s.21 refers merely to the proof of the power of attorney. Does an attested copy of a deposited instrument thus have an advantage over a certified copy power which has not been deposited?

Furnishing to purchaser of power relating to land

23.—A purchaser of any estate or interest in land is entitled to have any instrument creating a power of attorney which affects title thereto, or a certified copy or attested copy thereof, furnished by the vendor to the purchaser free of expense.

General Note

It is noteworthy that this section is not restricted to cases where the vendor is selling under power of attorney. It would seem to apply to all cases where a power of attorney affects title to land.

Part IV

Miscellaneous

Laying of orders and regulations before Houses of Oireachtas

24.—Every order and regulation made under this Act shall be laid before each House of the Oireachtas as soon as may be after it is made and, if a resolution annulling the order or regulation is passed by either such House within the next subsequent twenty-one days on which the House has sat after the order or regulation is laid before it, the order or regulation shall be annulled accordingly but without prejudice to the validity of anything previously done thereunder.

General Note

This is the usual section relating to orders and regulations made under the Powers of Attorney Act 1996.

Repeals

[25.—Subject to section 20(3), each enactment specified in the Fourth Schedule is hereby repealed to the extent specified in the third column of that Schedule.]

General Note

The Fourth Schedule lists ss.46, 47 and 48 of the Conveyancing Act 1881 and ss.8 and

9 of the Conveyancing Act 1882.

This section was amended and replaced by s.5 of the Family Law (Miscellaneous Provisions) Act 1997 (No. 18 of 1997) which came into effect on 5 May 1997, and which provided for the substitution of the above section.

Sections 9, 10, 14 FIRST SCHEDULE

NOTIFICATION PRIOR TO REGISTRATION

PART I

Duty to give Notice to Donor and Other Persons

Duty to give Notice to Donor

1. (1) Subject to subparagraph (2), before making an application for registration the attorney shall give notice of intention to do so to the donor.

(2) Paragraph 4(2) shall apply in relation to the donor as it applies in relation to a person who is entitled to receive notice under this Schedule.

GENERAL NOTE

The form and contents of the notice to the donor are contained in para.5 (see below). Paragraph 4(2) permits the attorney, before applying for registration, to make an application to the court to be dispensed from the requirement to give notice (see below).

Duty to give Notice to Other Persons

2. (1) Subject to paragraph 4—

(a) if regulations under section 5(2) have required notice of the execution of an enduring power of attorney to be brought to the attention of specified persons, the attorney shall, before making an application for registration, give notice of intention to do so to those persons;

(b) if any of those persons is dead or mentally incapable or his or her whereabouts cannot be reasonably ascertained, the attorney shall give notice of intention to make such an application to the other person or persons, and

(c) if all those persons are dead or mentally incapable or their whereabouts cannot be reasonably ascertained, the attorney shall, before making such an application, give notice of intention to do so to the persons (if any) who are entitled to receive notice by virtue of paragraph 3.

(2) When giving notice pursuant to subparagraph (1) the attorney shall also give notice to the Registrar of Wards of Court of intention to apply to the court for registration of the enduring power.

GENERAL NOTE

It should be noted that Regulations have been made under s.5(2) (see S.I. No. 196 of 1996).

3. (1) Subject to the limitations contained in subparagraphs (2) to (4), persons of the following classes are entitled to receive notice under paragraph 2(1)(c):

(a) the donor's husband or wife;

[(aa) the donor's civil partner, within the meaning of the Civil Partnership and Certain Rights and Obligations of Cohabitants Act 2010;]

(b) the donor's children;
(c) the donor's parents;
(d) the donor's brothers and sisters, whether of the whole or half blood;
(e) the widow or widower of a child of the donor;
(f) the donor's grandchildren;
(g) the children of the donor's brothers and sisters of the whole blood;
(h) the children of the donor's brothers and sisters of the half [blood;]
[(i) the donor's qualified cohabitant, within the meaning of section 172 of the Civil Partnership and Certain Rights and Obligations of Cohabitants Act 2010.]

(2) A person is not entitled to receive notice under this paragraph if the name or address of that person is not known to and cannot be reasonably ascertained by the attorney.

(3) Except where subparagraph (4) applies, no more than three persons are entitled to receive notice by virtue of this paragraph and, in determining the persons who are so entitled, persons falling within class (a) of subparagraph (1) are to be preferred to persons falling within class (b) of that subparagraph, persons falling within class (b) are to be preferred to persons falling within class (c) of that subparagraph; and so on.

(4) Notwithstanding the limit of three specified in subparagraph (3), where—
(a) there is more than one person falling within any of classes (a) to (h) of subparagraph (1), and
(b) at least one of those persons would be entitled to receive notice by virtue of this paragraph,

then, subject to subparagraph (2), all the persons falling within that class are entitled to receive notice by virtue of this paragraph.

General Note

In the Bill as passed by the Seanad, only subparas 3(1)(a)–(d) were included. The remaining subparagraphs were added by the Dáil. It is interesting to note that, notwithstanding the provisions of s.5(7), an estranged spouse is still entitled to receive notice in preference to, in certain circumstances, the donor's parents, or brothers and sisters.

Paragraph 3(1)(aa) was inserted by s.104(4) of the Civil Partnership and Certain Rights and Obligations of Cohabitants Act 2010 (No. 24 of 2010), with the effect from 1 January 2011 (S.I. No. 648 of 2010).

Paragraph 3(1)(h) was amended and para.3(1)(i) inserted by s.205 of the Civil Partnership and Certain Rights and Obligations of Cohabitants Act 2010 (No. 24 of 2010), with effect from 1 January 2011 (S.I. No. 648 of 2010).

4. (1) An attorney shall not be required to give notice under paragraph 2 to himself or herself or to any other attorney under the power who is joining in making the application, notwithstanding that he or she or, as the case may be, the other attorney is entitled to receive notice by virtue of paragraph 3.

(2) In the case of any person who is entitled to receive notice under this Schedule, the attorney, before applying for registration, may make an application to the court to be dispensed from the requirement to give that person notice; and the court may grant the application if it is satisfied—
(a) that it would be undesirable or impracticable for the attorney to give such notice; or

(b) that no useful purpose is likely to be served by giving it.

General Note

Paragraph 4(1) relieves an attorney from giving notice to him or herself. Subparagraph (2) empowers an attorney to apply to the courts to be dispensed from the requirement to give notice either to the donor, or to any of the persons referred to in paras 2 and 3. The court may grant that application if it is satisfied either that it would be undesirable or impracticable for the attorney to give such notice, or that no useful purpose is likely to be served by giving it. Presumably, this would refer to a situation where the donor's spouse is estranged.

Part II

Contents of Notices

5. A notice to the donor under this Schedule—
   (a) shall be in the prescribed form or a form to the like effect;
   (b) shall state that the attorney proposes to make an application to the court for the registration of the instrument creating the enduring power in question; and
   (c) shall inform the donor that, whilst the instrument remains registered, any revocation of the power by the donor will be ineffective unless and until the revocation is confirmed by the court.

General Note

In the Bill as passed by the Seanad, the words "to the court", in para.5(b) of the Act, appeared as "to the Registrar of Wards of Court". It is unlikely that this change will make any difference in practice.

6. A notice to any other person under this Schedule—
   (a) shall be in the prescribed form or a form to the like effect;
   (b) shall contain the statement mentioned in paragraph 5(b));
   (c) shall inform the person to whom it is given that that person may object to the proposed registration by notice in writing to the Registrar of Wards of Court before the expiry of the period of five weeks beginning with the day on which the notice under this Schedule was so given; and
   (d) shall specify, as the grounds on which an objection to registration may be made, the grounds set out in section 10(3).

General Note

This paragraph refers to notices to any person other than the donor. It is noteworthy that while para.6(d) provides that a notice to any person other than the donor shall specify, as the grounds on which an objection to registration may be made, the grounds set out in s.10(3), there is no corresponding subparagraph in para.5 (the Act appears to be silent on any procedure for enabling the donor to object to registration).

7. In this Part, "prescribed" means prescribed by regulations which may be made by the Minister.

General Note

Regulations have been made by the Minister (see Appendix A, below, p.47).

Part III

Duty to give Notice to other Attorneys

8. (1) Subject to subparagraph (2), before making an application for registration an attorney under a joint and several power shall give notice of intention to do so to any other attorney under the power who is not joining in making the application; and paragraphs 4(2) and 6 shall apply in relation to attorneys entitled to receive notice by virtue of this paragraph as they apply in relation to persons entitled to receive notice under this Schedule.

(2) An attorney is not entitled to receive notice by virtue of this paragraph if his or her address is not known to and cannot be reasonably ascertained by the applying attorney.

General Note

Paragraph 8 imposes a duty on the attorney under a joint and several power, before making an application for registration, to give notice of intention to do so to any other attorney under the power who is not joining in making the application. Paragraphs 4(2) and (6) shall apply in relation to attorneys entitled to receive notice. Attorneys who are appointed, or are deemed to have been appointed to act jointly, must, by virtue of such appointment, apply jointly for registration.

Part IV

Supplementary

9. For the purposes of this Schedule a notice given by post may be sent by prepaid registered post to the usual or last known place of residence of the person to whom it is to be given and shall be regarded as given on the day on which it was posted.

General Note

This paragraph provides that a notice given by post may be sent by pre-paid registered post. The First Schedule does not provide a method for giving notice, nor is such a method specified by the regulations. However, if notice is given by pre-paid registered post, it shall be regarded as given on the day on which it was posted. No provision is made for a case where the notice is returned undelivered. It would, perhaps, have been wiser to have empowered the Minister to make Regulations in relation to the service of notice.

Section 14

SECOND SCHEDULE

Joint and Joint and Several Attorneys

Part I

Joint Attorneys

1. In section 5(4), the reference to the time when the attorney executes the instrument shall be read as a reference to the time when the second or last attorney executes the instrument.

General Note

Section 5(4) provides that a power of attorney cannot be an enduring power unless, when executing the instrument creating it, the attorney possesses certain qualifications, such as, having attained the age of 18 years.

2. In sections 5(5), 8, 10(3), 12(2) and 12(4), references to the attorney shall be read as including references to any attorney under the power and, in the case of section 12(4)(d), subject to section 14(3).

[2A. The expiry of an enduring power of attorney effected in the circumstances mentioned in section 5(7) shall apply only so far as it relates to an attorney who is the spouse of the donor.]

[2B. The expiry of an enduring power of attorney effected in the circumstances mentioned in section 5(7A) shall apply only so far as it relates to an attorney who is the civil partner of the donor.]

General Note

This paragraph applies the sections mentioned therein to any attorney appointed under the power.

Paragraph 2A was inserted by s.50 of the Family Law (Divorce) Act 1996 (No. 33 of 1996), which came into effect on 27 February 1996.

Paragraph 2B was inserted by s.104(5) of the Civil Partnership and Certain Rights and Obligations of Cohabitants Act 2010 (No. 24 of 2010), with effect from 1 January 2011 (S.I. No. 648 of 2010).

Part II

Joint and Several Attorneys

3. The expiry of an enduring power of attorney effected in the circumstances mentioned in section 5(7) shall apply only so far as it relates to an attorney who is the spouse of the donor.

[4. The expiry of an enduring power of attorney effected in the circumstances mentioned in section 5(7A) shall apply only so far as it relates to an attorney who is the civil partner of the donor.]

General Note

Section 5(7) provides that an enduring power in favour of a spouse shall, unless the power provides otherwise, be invalidated, or cease to be in force, if certain events occur subsequently, such as the annulment of the marriage. Paragraph 3 covers the situation where the spouse is a joint and several attorney, and thus s.5(7) shall apply only insofar as it relates to that spouse.

Paragraph 4 was inserted by s.104(6) of the Civil Partnership and Certain Rights and Obligations of Cohabitants Act 2010 (No. 24 of 2010), with effect from 1 January 2011 (S.I. No. 648 of 2010).

Section 16 THIRD SCHEDULE

FORM OF GENERAL POWER OF ATTORNEY

This GENERAL POWER OF ATTORNEY IS MADE THIS day of 19 by AB of
I appoint CD of
[or CD of and EF of jointly (or jointly and severally)] to be my attorney[s] in accordance with section 16 of the Powers of Attorney Act, 1996.

IN WITNESS etc.

Section 25 FOURTH SCHEDULE

ENACTMENTS REPEALED

Chapter	*Short Title*	*Extent of Repeal*
44 & 45 Vict., c. 41	Conveyancing Act, 1881	Part XI (sections 46, 47 and 48).
45 & 46 Vict., c. 39	Conveyancing Act, 1882	Sections 8 and 9.

APPENDIX A

ENDURING POWERS OF ATTORNEY REGULATIONS, 1996

(S.I. No. 196 of 1996)

I, Mervyn Taylor, Minister for Equality and Law Reform, in exercise of the powers conferred on me by section 5(2) of, and the First Schedule to, the Powers of Attorney Act, 1996 (No. 12 of 1996), hereby make the following regulations:

Citation

1. These Regulations may be cited as the Enduring Powers of Attorney Regulation

Commencement

2. These Regulations shall come into operation on the 1st day of August 1996.

Form of instrument creating enduring power

3. (a) An instrument creating an enduring power shall be in the form set out in the First Schedule to these Regulations or, if the instrument relates only to personal care decisions, in the form set out in the Second Schedule thereto.
   (b) It shall include all the explanatory information in Part A of the form and the statements in Parts D and E.

Execution

4. (a) The instrument shall be executed by both the donor and the attorney (who shall execute the instrument after the donor, but not necessarily on the same date), each in the presence of a witness, but not necessarily the same witness, who shall give his or her full name and address.
   (b) The donor shall not witness the signature of an attorney nor shall an attorney witness the signature of the donor or of another attorney.

Accounts

5. An attorney who is appointed to act on the donor's behalf in relation to property and affairs of the donor shall keep adequate accounts of the management thereof and, in particular, of any expenditure to meet the needs of persons other than the donor or to make any gifts authorised by the enduring power.

Remuneration of attorney

6. The instrument may make provision in relation to the remuneration of an attorney.[1]

---

[1] See Law Society of Ireland, *Enduring Powers of Attorney Guidelines for Solicitors*, para.2.7 (Appendix E).

Notice to specified persons of execution of enduring power

7. (a) Notice of the execution of the enduring power by the donor shall be given by or on behalf of the donor to at least two persons named by the donor in the enduring power.
(b) None of them shall be an attorney under the power.
(c) At least one of them shall be –
(i)the donor's spouse, if living with the donor, or
(ii)if clause (i) does not apply, a child of the donor, or
(iii)if clauses (i) and (ii) do not apply, a relative (if any) of the donor.
(d) In subparagraph (c)(iii) "relative" means a parent, brother or sister (whether of the whole or half blood) or grandchild of the donor, the widow or widower of a child of the donor or a child of the donor's brother or sister (whether of the whole or half blood).

Form of notice of execution by donor of enduring power

8. A notice of the execution of an enduring power by the donor shall be in the form set out in the Third Schedule to these Regulations.

Form of notice to donor and other persons of intention to apply for registration of enduring power

9. A notice by the attorney to the donor and other persons mentioned in paragraph 2 or 3 of the First Schedule to the Powers of Attorney Act, 1996, shall be in the form set out in the Fourth Schedule to these Regulations.

FIRST SCHEDULE

Instrument creating Enduring Power of Attorney

Prescribed Form

PART A: EXPLANATORY INFORMATION

[*Note:* 1. This Part may not be omitted from the instrument.
2. If the enduring power is to relate only to personal care decisions, the form in the Second Schedule should be used]

Notice to donor and attorneys

1. Following is a simplified explanation of what the Powers of Attorney Act 1996 provides. If you need any more guidance you or your advisers will need to look at the Act itself.

2. Do not sign this enduring power unless you understand what it means. If you are in any doubt you should obtain legal advice.

Effect of creating enduring power: information for donor

3. An enduring power of attorney enables you to choose a person (called an "attorney") to manage your property and affairs in the event of your becoming

mentally incapable of doing so. You may choose one attorney or more than one. If you choose more than one, you must decide whether they are to be able to act:

> **jointly** (that is, they must all act together and cannot act separately), or **jointly and severally** (that is, they can all act together but they can also act separately if they wish).

In Part B of this document, at the place marked [1], show what you have decided by crossing out or omitting one of the alternatives. If you do not, the attorneys are deemed to have been appointed to act jointly.

4. If you give your attorney(s) general power in relation to all your property and affairs, they will be able to deal with your money or property and may be able to sell your house.

5. If you do not want your attorney(s) to have such wide powers, you can include any restrictions you like. For example, you can include a restriction that your attorney(s) may not sell your house. Any restrictions you choose must be written or typed at the place marked [2] in Part B of this document.

6. You may authorise the attorney(s) to take certain personal care decisions on your behalf, e.g. deciding where you shall live. If you decide to do so, you should indicate, at the place marked [3] in Part B of this document, the particular personal care decisions you want to authorise. You should also name any person you would like the attorney to consult so that the attorney can have regard to that person's views as to your wishes and feelings and as to what would be in your best interests.

7. Unless you put in a restriction preventing it, your attorney(s) will be able to use any of your money or property to benefit themselves or other people by doing what you yourself might be expected to do to provide for their needs.

8. If you specifically authorise it, your attorney(s) will also be able to use your money to make gifts, but only for reasonable amounts in relation to the value of your money and property and subject to any conditions or restrictions you may impose.

9. You may also appoint an attorney or attorneys to act in the event that the original attorney is unable or unwilling to act. Provision for such an appointment is made at the place marked [4] in Part B of this document.

10. You must give notice of the execution of the enduring power as soon as practicable to at least two persons. None of them may be an attorney under the power. At least one must be the donor's spouse, if living with the donor. If the donor is unmarried, widowed or separated, notification must be given to a child of the donor (if applicable) or otherwise to any relative (i.e. parent, sibling, grandchild, widow/er of child, nephew or niece). You should give the names and addresses of those notified at the place marked [5] in Part B of this document. The prescribed form of notice is contained in the Third Schedule to the Enduring Powers of Attorney Regulations, 1996.

11. Your attorney(s) can recover the out-of-pocket expenses of acting as

your attorney(s). You may provide for the attorney's remuneration as well at the place marked [6] in Part B of this document.

12. If your attorney(s) have reason in the future to believe that you have become or are becoming mentally incapable of managing your affairs, your attorney(s) must apply to have the enduring power registered in the High Court. Once registered, an enduring power of attorney cannot be revoked effectively unless the Court confirms the revocation. You may revoke the power at any time before registration.

13. Before applying to registration of this power, your attorney(s) must give written notice of intention to do so to you and to the persons you notify of the execution of the enduring power. You and these persons (if they are not then available, certain of your relatives) will be able to object if you or they disagree with registration. The prescribed form of notice is contained in the Fourth Schedule to the Enduring Powers of Attorney Regulations, 1996.

Effect of accepting enduring power: information for attorney

14. If you have reason in the future to believe that the donor is, or is becoming, mentally incapable of managing his or her property and affairs, you must apply to have the enduring power registered in the High Court. Before doing so you must give written notice of your intention to the Registrar of Wards of Court and also to the donor and the persons whom the donor has notified of the execution of the enduring power. (If these persons are no longer available, notice must be given to certain relatives, as specified in the Powers of Attorney Act 1996.) The prescribed form of the latter notice is contained in the Fourth Schedule to the Enduring Powers of Attorney Regulations, 1996.

15. The enduring power will not come into force until it has been registered. However, once you have applied for registration you may take action under the power to maintain the donor and prevent loss to the donor's estate and maintain yourself and other persons in so far as that is permitted under section 6(4) of the Act. You may also make any personal care decisions permitted under the power that cannot reasonably be deferred until the application for registration has been determined.

16. Unless there is a restriction in the enduring power preventing it, you may use the donor's money or other property for your benefit or that of other people to the following extent but no further, that is to say, by doing what the donor might be expected to do to provide for your or their needs. You may not use the donor's money to make gifts unless there is specific provision to that effect in the enduring power and then only to persons related to or connected with the donor on birth or marriage anniversaries or to charities to which the donor made or might be expected to make gifts. The amounts of any such gifts are subject to any restrictions in the enduring power and, in any event, may be only for reasonable amounts in relation to the extent of the donor's assets.

17. You are obliged to keep adequate accounts of the donor's property and affairs and to produce the accounting records to the Court if required.

18. In general, as an attorney you are in a fiduciary relationship with the donor. You must use proper care in exercising on behalf of the donor the authority given by the enduring power and you must act only within its scope. In particular, you must observe any conditions or restrictions imposed by the power and also the limits imposed by the Powers of Attorney Act, 1996.

19. You may recover the out-of-pocket expenses of acting as attorney. The enduring power may provide for remuneration for so acting.

20. You may disclaim at any time up to registration of the power. Thereafter you may do so only on notice to the donor and with the consent of the High Court.

21. After the enduring power has been registered you should notify the Registrar of Wards of Court if the donor dies or recovers.

PART B: [TO BE COMPLETED BY THE "DONOR" (THE PERSON APPOINTING THE ATTORNEY(S))]

Do not sign this form unless you understand what it means. If you are in any doubt you should obtain legal advice.

[Donor's name and address	I, ________________ of ________________
Donor's date of birth	born on ________________
Name(s) and address(es) of attorney(s)	appoint ________________
See note 1 in Part A of this form. If you are appointing only one attorney you should cross out everything between the square brackets.	of ________________ [and ________________ of ________________
*Delete the one which does not apply (see note 1 in Part A of this form).	[l]*jointly *jointly and severally]
	to act as attorney(s) for the purpose of Part II of the Powers of Attorney Act, 1996
*Delete the one which does not apply (see note 2 in Part A of this form).	*with general authority to act on my behalf
If you do not want the attorney(s) to have general power, you must give details here of what authority you are giving the attorney(s).	*with authority to do the following on my behalf: in relation to
*Delete the one which does not apply.	*all my property and affairs
If you choose the second alternative you must give details here of the property and affairs in relation to which the power is	*the following property and affairs

to apply.

If there are restrictions or conditions, insert them here; if not, delete these words (see note 5 in Part Aof this document).

[[2] subject to the following restrictions and conditions:]

*[[3] and with authority to take on my behalf decisions on the following matters:

*where I should live

*with whom I should live

*whom I should see and not see

*what training or rehabilitation I should receive

*my diet and dress

*inspection of my personal papers

*Delete if not applicable.

*housing, social services and other benefits for me.]

*[____________ [and ________] should be consulted for his/her/their views as to wishes and feelings and as to what would be in my best interests.]

[[4] I appoint ________________

of ____________________________

[and __________________________

of ____________________________

*Delete this provision if, or to the extent, not required.

*jointly
*jointly and severally]

to act as attorney(s) if an attorney appointed by this instrument dies or is unable or declines to act or is disqualified from acting as attorney.]

[5] I am required to give notice of the execution of this power to at least two persons. I shall notify the following persons accordingly:

____

The two or more persons to be notified may not include an attorney under the power.

of ____________________________

____

One must be a person selected as mentioned in note 10 of Part A of this document.

____
of ____________________
____

____
of ____________________
____

*Delete if not applicable

*[6] My attorney(s) may be paid the following remuneration:

I intend this power to be effective during any subsequent mental incapacity of mine.

I have read or have had read to me the information in paragraphs 1 to 13 of Part A of this document.

Your signature

Date

Signed by me on ____________________

Signature of witness

In the presence of ____________

Your attorney(s) cannot be your witness. If you are married it is not advisable for your husband or wife to be your witness.]

Full name of witness ________

Address of witness ________

____
____
____
____
____

[*Note* – Anything in this Part in square brackets is for guidance only and may be retained, deleted or omitted as appropriate.]

PART C: [TO BE COMPLETED BY THE ATTORNEY(S)]

[This form may be adapted to provide for scaling by a trust corporation with its common seal.]

[If there are more than two attorneys attach an additional Part C.]

Do not sign this form unless you understand what it means. If you are in any doubt you should obtain legal advice. Do not sign the form before the donor has signed Part B.

I understand my duties and obligations as attorney, including my duty to apply to the High Court for the registration of this instrument under the Powers of Attorney Act, 1996, when the donor is, or is becoming, mentally incapable, my limited power to use the donor's property to benefit persons other than the donor and my obligation to keep adequate accounts in relation to the management and disposal of the donor's property for production to the High Court if required.

I have read or have had read to me the information in paragraphs 1, 2 and 14 to 21 of Part A of this document.

[Individuals disqualified from acting as attorney are bankrupts, persons convicted of certain offences or disqualified under the Companies Acts or owning or connected with the management or operation of a nursing home in which the donor resides.

I am not a minor or otherwise disqualified from acting as attorney.

Signature of attorney ______________________________

Date on ______________________________

Signature of witness in the presence of ____________________

Full name of witness ____________________

Address of witness ____________________

____

____

Each attorney must sign the form and each signature must be witnessed. The donor may not be the witness and one attorney may not witness the signature of another.]

[To be completed only if there is a second attorney

[I understand my duties and obligations as attorney, including my duty to apply to the High Court for the registration of this instrument under the Powers of Attorney Act 1996, when the donor is, or is becoming, mentally incapable, my limited power to use the donor's property to benefit persons other than the donor and my obligation to keep adequate accounts in relation to the management and disposal of the donor's property for production to the High Court if required.

	I have read or have had read to me the information in paragraphs 1, 2 and 14 to 21 of Part A of this document.
	I am not a minor or otherwise disqualified from acting as attorney.
Signature of attorney	______________________
Date	on ______________________
Signature of witness	in the presence of ______________
	Full name of witness______________
Each attorney must sign the form and each signature must be witnessed. The donor may not be the witness and one attorney may not witness the signature of another.]	Address of witness ______________ ______________________ ______________________ ______________________]
[To be completed only if the donor is appointing a person to act as attorney if an original attorney is unable or unwilling to act.	[I understand my duties and obligations if I have to act as attorney, including my duty to apply to the High Court for the registration of this instrument under the Powers of Attorney Act, 1996, when the donor is, or is becoming, mentally incapable, my limited powers to use the donor's property to benefit persons other than the donor and my obligation to keep adequate accounts in relation to the management and disposal of the donor's property for production to the High Court if required.
	I have read or have had read to me the information in paragraphs 1, 2 and 14 to 21 of Part A of this document.
Signature	______________________
Date	on______________________
Signature of witness]	in the presence of ______________
	Full name of witness______________]

[To be completed only if a second person is being so appointed.	[I understand my duties and obligations if I have to act as attorney, including my duty to apply to the High Court for the registration of this instrument under the Powers of Attorney Act, 1996, when the donor is, or is becoming, mentally incapable, my limited powers to use the donor's property to benefit persons other than the donor and my obligation to keep adequate accounts in relation to the management and disposal of the donor's property for production to the High Court if required. I have read or have had read to me the information in paragraphs 1, 2 and 14 to 21 of Part A of this document.
Signature	______________________
Date	on______________________
Signature of witness]	in the presence of ______________
	Full name of witness______________]

[***Note*** – Anything in this Part in square brackets is for guidance only and may be retained, deleted or omitted as appropriate.]

PART D: Statement by solicitor

*Delete if enquiries not necessary.	I, ______________________, Solicitor, of ______________hereby state that after interviewing the donor [and making any necessary enquiries]* I am satisfied that ____________ (the donor) understood the effect of creating the enduring power and I have no reason to believe that this document is being executed by the donor as a result of fraud or undue pressure. Signed ______________________ Date ______________________

[***Note*** – This Part may not be omitted from the instrument.]

PART E: Statement by Registered Medical Practitioner

*Name of donor	I, _____________, a registered medical practitioner, of _____________ hereby state that in my opinion at the time this document was executed by the donor ________________* had the mental capacity, with the assistance of such explanations as may have been given to the donor, to understand the effect of creating the power. Signed ______________________________ Date ________________________________

[***Note*** – This Part may not be omitted from the instrument.]

SECOND SCHEDULE

Instrument creating Enduring Power of Attorney
(personal care decisions only)

Prescribed Form

PART A: EXPLANATORY INFORMATION
[*Note* – This Part may not be omitted from the instrument.]

Notice to donor and attorneys

1. Following is a simplified explanation of what the Powers of Attorney Act, 1996 provides. If you need any more guidance you or your advisers will need to look at the Act itself.

2. Do not sign this enduring power unless you understand what it means. If you are in any doubt you should obtain legal advice.

Effect of creating enduring power: information for donor

3. This form of enduring power of attorney enables you to choose a person (called an "attorney") to make certain personal care decisions on your behalf in the event of your becoming mentally incapable. You may choose one attorney or more than one. If you choose more than one, you must decide whether they are to be able to act:

> **jointly** (that is, they must all act together and cannot act separately), or
> **jointly and severally** (that is, they can all act together but they can also act separately if they wish).

In Part B of this document, at the place marked [1], show what you have decided by crossing out or omitting one of the alternatives. If you do not, the attorneys are deemed to have been appointed jointly.

4. The personal care decisions that you may authorise your attorney(s) to make on your behalf are as follows:

> where you should live
> with whom you should live
> whom you should see and not see
> what training or rehabilitation you should get
> your diet and dress
> inspection of your personal papers
> housing, social welfare and other benefits for you.

5. You should indicate, at the place marked [2] in Part B of this document, the particular personal care decisions you want to authorise. You should also name any person you would like the attorney to consult so that the attorney can have regard to that person's views as to your wishes and feelings and as to what would be in your best interests.

6. You may also appoint an attorney or attorneys to act in the event that the

original attorney is unable or unwilling to act. Provision for such an appointment is made at the place marked [3] in Part B of this document.

7. You must give notice of the execution of the enduring power as soon as practicable to at least two persons. None of them may be an attorney under the power. At least one must be the donor's spouse, if living with the donor. If the donor is unmarried, widowed or separated, notification must be given to a child of the donor (if applicable) or otherwise to any relative (i.e. parent, sibling, grandchild, widow/er of child, nephew or niece. You should give the names and addresses of those notified at the place marked [4] in Part B of this document. The prescribed form of notice is contained in the Third Schedule to the Enduring Powers of Attorney Regulations, 1996.

8. Your attorney(s) can recover the out-of-pocket expenses of acting as your attorney(s). You may provide for the attorney's remuneration, and who is to pay it, at the place marked [5] in Part B of this document.

9. If your attorney(s) have reason in the future to believe that you have become or are becoming mentally incapable of managing your affairs, your attorney(s) must apply to have the enduring power registered in the High Court. Once registered, an enduring power of attorney cannot be revoked effectively unless the Court confirms the revocation. You may revoke the power at any time before registration.

10. Before applying for registration of this power, your attorney(s) must give written notice of intention to do so to you and to the persons you notify of the execution of the enduring power. You and these persons (if they are not then available, certain of your relatives) will be able to object if you or they disagree with registration. The prescribed form of notice is contained in the Fourth Schedule to the Enduring Powers of Attorney Regulations, 1996.

Effect of accepting enduring power: information for attorney

11. If you have reason in the future to believe that the donor is, or is becoming, mentally incapable of managing his or her property and affairs, you must apply to have the enduring power registered in the High Court. Before doing so you must give written notice of your intention to the Registrar of Wards of Court and also to the donor and the persons whom the donor has notified of the execution of the enduring power. (If these persons are no longer available, notice must be given to certain relatives, as specified in the Powers of Attorney Act 1996.) The prescribed form of the latter notice is contained in the Fourth Schedule to the Enduring Powers of Attorney Regulations, 1996.

12. The enduring power will not come into force until it has been registered. However, once you have applied for registration you may make any personal care decisions permitted under the power that cannot reasonably be deferred until the application for registration has been determined.

13. Any personal decision you make on behalf of the donor must be made in the donor's best interests. Section 6(7)(b) of the 1996 Act provides the following guidance in this respect:

"In deciding what is in a donor's best interests regard shall be had to the following:

(i) so far as ascertainable, the past and present wishes and feelings of the donor and the factors which the donor would consider if he or she were able to do so;

(ii) the need to permit and encourage the donor to participate, or to improve the donor's ability to participate, as fully as possible in any decision affecting the donor;

(iii) so far as it is practicable and appropriate to consult any of the persons mentioned below, their views as to the donor's wishes and feelings and as to what would be in the donor's best interests:

(I) any person named by the donor as someone to be consulted on those matters;

(II) anyone (whether the donor's spouse, a relative, friend or other person) engaged in caring for the donor or interested in the donor's welfare;

(iv) whether the purpose for which any decision is required can be as effectively achieved in a manner less restrictive of the donor's freedom of action."

Section 6(7) further provides that in the case of any personal care decision made by an attorney it shall be a sufficient compliance with this provision if the attorney reasonably believes that what he or she decides is in the best interests of the donor.

14. You may recover the out-of-pocket expenses of acting as attorney. The enduring power may provide for remuneration for so acting.

15. You may disclaim at any time up to registration of the power. Thereafter you may do so only on notice to the donor and with the consent of the High Court.

16. After the enduring power has been registered you should notify the Registrar of Wards of Court if the donor dies or recovers.

PART B: [TO BE COMPLETED BY THE "DONOR" (THE PERSON APPOINTING THE ATTORNEY(S))]

Do not sign this form unless you understand what it means. If you are in any doubt you should obtain legal advice.

[Donor's name and address	I, ______________________
	of______________________
Donor's date of birth	born on ______________________
Name(s) and address(es) of attorney(s)	appoint______________________
	of______________________
	[and______________________

See note 3 in Part A of this document If you are appointing only one attorney you should delete everything between the square brackets.	of ______________________________
*Delete the one which does not apply (see note 3 in Part A of this document).	[l]*jointly *jointly and severally] to act as attorney[s] for the purposes of Part II of the Powers of Attorney Act, 1996 [2] with authority to take on my behalf decisions on the following matters:
*Delete if not applicable.	*where I should live *with whom I should live *whom I should see and not see *what training or rehabilitation I should get *my diet and dress *inspection of my personal papers *housing, social services and other benefits for me.] *[___________ [and__________] should be consulted for his/her/their views as to my wishes and feelings and as to what would be in my best interests.]
Delete this provision if, or to the extent, not required.	[[3] I appoint ____________________ of ______________________________ [and ____________________________ of ______________________________ *jointly *jointly and severally] to act as attorney(s) if an attorney appointed by this instrument disclaims or dies or is unable to act or is disqualified from acting as attorney.]
	[4] I am required to give notice of the execution of this power to at least two persons. I shall notify the following persons accordingly: ________________________________ of ______________________________ ________________________________

The two or more persons to be notified may not include an attorney under the power. One must be a person selected as mentioned in note 7 of Part A of this document.	________ of________ ________ ________ of________ ________
*Delete if not applicable.	*[5] My attorney(s) may be paid the following remuneration: ________
Name of payer	by________]
	I intend that this power shall continue even if I become mentally incapable.[2]
	I have read or have had read to me the information in paragraphs 1 to 10 of Part A of this document.
Your signature Date	Signed by me on________
	In the presence of ________
Someone must witness your signature	Full name of witness Address of witness ________
Your attorney(s) cannot be your witness. If you are married it is not advisable for your husband or wife to be your witness.]	________ ________ ________

[*Note* – Anything in this Part in square brackets is for guidance only and may be retained, deleted or omitted as appropriate.]

PART C: [TO BE COMPLETED BY THE ATTORNEY(S)]

[This form may be adapted to provide for sealing by a trust corporation with its common seal.]

[If there are more than two attorneys attach an additional Part C.]

Do not sign this form unless you understand what it means. If you are in any doubt you should obtain legal advice. Do not sign the form before the donor has signed Part B.

---

[2] Note the amendment of this provision by S.I. No. 287 of 1996, Appendix B, p.69 of this text.

I understand my duties and obligations as attorney, including my duty to apply to the High Court for the registration of this instrument under the Powers of Attorney Act, 1996, when the donor is, or is becoming, mentally incapable, and that any personal care decisions made by me on behalf of the donor must be made in the donor's best interests.

[Individuals disqualified from acting as attorney are bankrupts, persons convicted of certain offences or disqualified under the Companies Acts or owning or connected with the management or operation of a nursing home in which the donor resides.

I have read or have had read to me the information in paragraphs 1, 2 and 11 to 16 of Part A of this document.

I am not a minor or otherwise disqualified from acting as attorney.

Signature of attorney ______________________________

Date ______________________________

Signature of witness in the presence of ______________

Full name of witness ______________

Address of witness ______________

____

____

____

Each attorney must sign the form and each signature must be witnessed. The donor may not be the witness and one attorney may not witness the signature of another.]

[To be completed only if there is a second attorney.

I understand my duties and obligations as attorney, including my duty to apply to the High Court for the registration of this instrument under the Powers of Attorney Act, 1996, when the donor is, or is becoming, mentally incapable, and that any personal care decisions made by me on behalf of the donor must be made in the donor's best interests.

I have read or have had read to me the information in paragraphs 1, 2 and 11 to 16 of Part A of this document.

See note above regarding disqualified persons.

I am not a minor or otherwise disqualified persons.

Signature of attorney ______________________________

Date ______________________________

Signature of witness in the presence of ______________

Full name of witness ______________

Each attorney must sign the form and each signature must be witnessed. The donor may not be the witness and one attorney may not witness the signature of another.]

Address of witness ______________

____

____

____

[To be completed only if the donor is appointing a person to act as attorney if an original attorney is unable or unwilling to act

[I understand my duties and obligations if I have to act as attorney, including my duty to apply to the High Court for the registration of this instrument under the Attorrney Act, 1996, when the donor is, or is becoming, mentally incapable, and that any personal care decisions made by me on the donor's behalf must be made in the donor's best interests.

I have read or have had read to me the information in paragraphs 1, 2 and 11 to 16 of Part A of this document.

See note above regarding disqualified persons.

I am not a minor or otherwise disqualified from acting as attorney.

Signature ________________________________

Date on____________________________

Signature of witness] in the presence of ______________

Full name of witness______________

Address of witness ______________]

[To be completed only if a second person is being so appointed.

[I understand my duties and obligations if I have to act as attorney, including my duty to apply to the High Court for the registration of this instrument under the Powers of Attorney Act, 1996, when the donor is, or is becoming, mentally incapable, and that any personal care decisions made by me on the donor's behalf must be made in the donor's best interests.

I have read or have had read to me the information in paragraphs 1, 2 and 11 to 16 of Part A of this document.

See note above regarding disqualified persons.

I am not a minor or otherwise disqualified from acting as attorney.

Signature ________________________________

Date on____________________________

Signature of witness] in the presence of ______________

Full name of witness______________

Address of witness _____________]

[***Note*** – Anything in this Part in square brackets is for guidance only and may be retained, deleted or omitted as appropriate.]

PART D: Statement by Solicitor

*Delete if enquiries not necessary.

I, ____________________, Solicitor, of ________________ hereby state that after interviewing the donor [and making any necessary enquiries]* I am satisfied that _______________ (the donor) understood the effect of creating the enduring power and I have no reason to believe that this document is being executed by the donor as a result of fraud or undue pressure.

Signed ___________________________

Date _____________________________

[***Note*** – This Part may not be omitted from the instrument.]

PART E: Statement by Registered Medical Practitioner

*Name of donor

I, _______________, a registered medical practitioner, of ________ hereby state that in my opinion at the time this document was executed by the donor _________________* had the mental capacity, with the assistance of such explanations as may have been given to the donor, to understand the effect of creating the power.

Signed ___________________________

Date _____________________________

[***Note*** – This Part may not be omitted from the instrument.]

THIRD SCHEDULE

ENDURING POWERS OF ATTORNEY REGULATIONS, 1996

Notice of execution by donor of enduring power

	To ______________________________
	of ______________________________
[Name of donor	TAKE NOTICE that I, ______________________
Address of donor	of ______________________________
	executed on ______________ 19 ____ an instrument creating an enduring power of attorney and appointing
Name of attorney	______________________________
Address of attorney	of ______________________________
	______________________________
Delete words in brackets if you have appointed only one attorney	[and ______________________________
	of ______________________________]
	to act as my attorney(s) if I should become mentally incapacitated.
Signature of donor]	Signed ______________________________
	Date ______________________________

Information for donor

1. You must give notice of the execution of the enduring power to at least two people.

2. None of the persons to be notified may be an attorney under the enduring power.

3. At least one must be your spouse, if living with you. If you are unmarried, widowed or separated, notification must be given to your child (if applicable) or otherwise to any relative (i.e. parent, sibling, grandchild, widow/er of child, nephew or niece).

4. It is advisable that this notice be sent by prepaid registered post and that the certificate of posting be kept in a safe place.

Information for recipient of notice

1. The enduring power will not come into force until the donor is, or is becoming, mentally incapable of managing his or her property and affairs and until it has been registered in the High Court.

2. Notice of intention to apply for registration of the enduring power will be given to you before the attorney applies for registration.

[***Note*** – The words in square brackets in the margin of the form may be omitted.]

FOURTH SCHEDULE

ENDURING POWERS OF ATTORNEY REGULATIONS, 1996

Notice of intention to apply for registration

	To ____
	of ____
Name of attorney(s)	TAKE NOTICE that I/we ________________________ ____
Address(es) of attorney(s)	of ____ ____ ____ ____
Name of donor	the attorney(s) of ____________________________
Address of donor	(hereinafter called "the donor") of____________________ ____ ____

propose to apply to the High Court for the registration of the instrument creating the enduring power of attorney appointing me/us attorney(s) and executed by the donor on the ____ 19__.

1. You have 5 weeks from the date on which this notice is given to object in writing to the proposed registration of the enduring power. Objections should be sent to the Registrar of Wards of Court, Four Courts, Dublin 7 and should contain the following details:

(a) your name and address,

(b) if you are not the donor, the name and address of the donor,

(c) any relationship to the donor,

(d) the name and address of the attorney, and

(e) the grounds for objecting to the registration of the enduring power.

2. You may object to the registration of the enduring power on any one or more of the following grounds:

(a) that the enduring power purported to have been created was not valid;

(b) that the enduring power is no longer a valid and subsisting power;

(c) that the donor is not, or is not becoming, mentally incapable;

(d) that, having regard to all the circumstances, the attorney is unsuitable to be the donor's attorney;

(e) that fraud or undue pressure was used to induce the donor to create the enduring power.

Delete this paragraph if the notice is addressed to a person other than the donor.	3. You are informed that while the enduring power remains registered you will not be able to revoke it unless and until the Court confirms the revocation.
The notice should be signed by all the attorneys who are applying to register the enduring power.	Signed ________________ Signed ________________ Date ________________

Notice to attorney(s):

1. This notice must be given to the donor and also to the other persons who were notified of the execution of the enduring power and are named in it.
2. If any of those persons are dead or mentally incapable or their whereabouts cannot be reasonably ascertained, the notice must be given to the other person or persons who were so notified.
3. If all of those persons are dead or mentally incapable or their whereabouts cannot be reasonably ascertained, the notice must be given to the relatives (if any) who are entitled to receive notice by virtue of paragraph 3 of the First Schedule of the Powers of Attorney Act 1996.
4. You must also give notice to the Registrar of Wards of Court of your intention to apply to the Court for registration of the power at the same time as you are giving notice to the donor and those other persons. A copy of each of the notices should be enclosed for the Registrar's information.

[*Note* – The words in square brackets in the margin of the form may be omitted.]

APPENDIX B

ENDURING POWERS OF ATTORNEY
(PERSONAL CARE DECISIONS) REGULATIONS, 1996
(S.I. No. 287 of 1996)

I, Mervyn Taylor, Minister for Equality and Law Reform, in exercise of the powers conferred on me by section 5(2) of the Powers of Attorney Act, 1996 (No. 12 of 1996), hereby make the following regulations:

1. These Regulations may be cited as the Enduring Powers of Attorney (Personal Care Decisions) Regulations, 1996.

2. These Regulations shall come into operation on the 7th day of October, 1996.

3. (1) The Enduring Powers of Attorney Regulations, 1996 (S.I. No. 196 of 1996), are hereby amended by the deletion from Part B of the Second Schedule of the sentence "I intend that this power shall continue even if I become mentally incapable" and the substitution of the following: "I intend this power to be effective during any subsequent mental incapacity of mine.".

(2) The said Part B, as so amended, is set out for convenience in the Annex to these Regulations.

(3) The said amendment is made without prejudice to the validity of the original form contained in instruments made before the commencement of these Regulations.

ANNEX

SECOND SCHEDULE, ENDURING POWERS OF ATTORNEY
REGULATIONS, 1996, NEW PART B

PART B: [TO BE COMPLETED BY THE "DONOR" (THE PERSON APPOINTING THE ATTORNEY(S))]

Do not sign this form unless you understand what it means. If you are in any doubt you should obtain legal advice.

[Donor's name and address	I, ______________________
	of______________________
Donor's date of birth	born on ________________
Name(s) and address(es) of attorney(s)	appoint__________________
See note 3 in Part A of this document. If appointing only one attorney you should delete everything between the square brackets.	[and ____________________ ________________________
*Delete the one which does not apply (see note 3 in Part A of this document).	[l]*jointly *jointly and severally]

to act as attorney[s] for the purposes of Part II of the Powers of Attorney Act, 1996

[2] with authority to take on my behalf decisions on the following matters:

	*where I should live
Delete if not applicable.	*with whom I should live
	*whom I should see and not see *what training or rehabilitation I should get *my diet and dress *inspection of my personal papers *housing, social services and other benefits for me. *[___________ [and_________] should be consulted for his/her/their views as to my wishes and feelings and as to what would be in my best interests.]
Delete this provision if, or to the extent, not required.	[[3] I appoint__________________ of___________________________ [and __________________________ of___________________________ *jointly *jointly and severally] to act as attorney(s) if an attorney appointed by this instrument disclaims or dies or is unable to act or is disqualified from acting as attorney.]
	[4] I am required to give notice of the execution of this power to at least two persons. I shall notify the following persons accordingly: ____________________________ of__________________________ ____________________________
The two or more persons to be notified may not include an attorney under the power. One must be a person selected as mentioned in note 7 of Part A of this document.	____________________________ of__________________________ ____________________________
	____________________________ of__________________________ ____________________________

*Delete if not applicable.	*[[5] My attorney(s) may be paid the following remuneration: ______________________________
Name of payer	by ____________________________.]
	I intend this power to be effective during any subsequent mental incapacity of mine.
	I have read or have had read to me the information in paragraphs 1 to 10 of Part A of this document.
Your signature	Signed by me____________________
Date	on____________________________
	In the presence of _______________
Someone must witness your signature.	Full name of witness_____________
	Address of witness ______________
Your attorney(s) cannot be your witness. If you are married it is not advisable for your husband or wife to be your witness.]	______________________________ ______________________________ ______________________________

[***Note*** – Anything in this Part in square brackets is for guidance only and may be retained, deleted or omitted as appropriate.]

APPENDIX C

RULES OF THE SUPERIOR COURTS (No. 1)
(POWERS OF ATTORNEY ACT, 1996) 2000 (S.I. No. 66 of 2000)

1. The following Order shall be inserted as Order 129 of the Rules of the Superior Courts immediately after Order 128 thereof.

2. This rule shall come into operation on the 8th day of March 2000.

3. This rule shall be construed with the Rules of the Superior Courts, 1986 to 2000 and may be cited as the Rules of the Superior Courts (No. 1) (Powers of Attorney Act, 1996) 2000.

ORDER 129

POWERS OF ATTORNEY ACT, 1996

1. In this Order—

"the Act" means the Powers of Attorney Act, 1996.

"the Court" means the President of the High Court or such other Judge of the High Court as may be assigned by him from time to time to hear applications under the Act and shall, where appropriate, include the Registrar.

"the Registrar" means the Registrar of Wards of Court.

"the Regulations" means the Enduring Powers of Attorney Regulations, 1996 (S.I. No. 196 of 1996) as amended by the Enduring Powers of Attorney (Personal Care Decisions) Regulations, 1996 (S.I. No. 287 of 1996).

Words and expressions shall, unless the contrary intention appears, have the same meaning as in the Act.

Pre-Registration Applications

2.(1) The following applications may be made *ex parte* to the Court by means of an *ex parte* docket:

(a) an application pursuant to section 8 of the Act for the exercise of any power created under an enduring power of attorney prior to the registration of the instrument creating such power,

(b) an application pursuant to section 9(3) of the Act referring to the Court for its determination any question as to the validity of the power;

(c) an application pursuant to paragraph 4(2) of the First Schedule to the Act to dispense with the requirement to give notice of intention to make an application for registration under section 9 of the Act.

(2) An *ex parte* application shall be grounded upon the affidavit of the interested party or the attorney, as the case may be, and shall be lodged in the Office of the Wards of Court and shall fully set forth the facts and circumstances giving rise to the application. In particular the affidavit shall contain the

following matters:

(a) the present address of the donor;

(b) the present address or addresses of the person or persons to whom notice of execution of the power has been given;

(c) the date on which the enduring power of attorney was executed;

(d) the date on which notice of execution by the donor was given;

(e) the date of completion of the statement by the attorney prescribed by Part C of the Form in the First or Second Schedule to the Regulations, as the case may be;

(f) the date of completion of the statement by the solicitor prescribed by Part D of the Form in the First or Second Schedule to the Regulations, as the case may be;

(g) the date of completion of the statement by the doctor prescribed by Part E of the Form required by the First or Second Schedule to the Regulations, as the case may be;

(h) the date on which notice of intention to apply for registration was given to the donor, (if applicable);

(i) the date or dates upon which notice of intention to apply for registration was given to the required notice parties prescribed by the Act or Regulations, (if applicable),

and the affidavit shall exhibit the power of attorney concerned and all other relevant documentation.

(3) The Court may upon such application make such order as appears appropriate in the circumstances including an order adjourning the application and directing that notice of the application be served upon any person likely to be affected thereby or may adjourn such application until it makes or causes to be made such enquiries or further enquiries, if any, as it thinks appropriate in the circumstances of the case and upon such terms and conditions as appear just.

Application for Registration

3.(1) An application for the registration of an enduring power of attorney shall be made to the Registrar by lodging an application for registration in the Office of the Wards of Court and shall be grounded upon the affidavit of the attorney or attorneys seeking such registration. Such application shall, as far as practicable, be in the Form No. 1 as set out in the Appendix hereto.

(2) An affidavit grounding such an application shall fully set forth the facts and circumstances giving rise to the application. In particular the affidavit shall contain the following matters:

(a) the present address and marital status of the donor;

(b) the present address or addresses (if known) of the person or persons to whom notice of execution of the power has been given;

(c) the date on which the enduring power of attorney was executed (if known);

(d) the date on which notice of execution by the donor was given (if known);

(e) the date of completion of the statement by the attorney prescribed in

Part C of the Form in the First or Second Schedule to the Regulations, as the case may be;

(f) the date of the completion of the statement by the solicitor prescribed by Part D of the Form in the First or Second Schedule to the Regulations, as the case may be;

(g) the date of completion of the statement by the doctor prescribed by Part E of the form required by the First or Second Schedule to the Regulations, as the case may be;

(h) the date upon which notice of intention to apply for registration was given to the donor;

(i) the date or dates upon which notice of intention to apply for registration was given to the Registrar and the required notice parties prescribed by the Act or Regulations;

(j) aver that the enduring power of attorney has not been interfered with or altered in any way since it came into the possession of the attorney and shall aver as to the date and manner in which it came into the possession of the attorney concerned;

(k) a statement that a registered medical practitioner has certified that the donor is or is becoming incapable of managing and administering his or her own property and affairs;

(l) that there is no other person to whom notice is required to be given by virtue of the provisions of the First Schedule to the Act;

and the application shall have annexed to it the power of attorney concerned, any medical certificate issued pursuant to section 9(4) of the Act, any relevant notices (or copies thereof, if available), referred to above and any other relevant documentation.

(3) The application for registration shall be served on the donor personally and on all other parties who either have or should have received notice of an intention to apply for registration. Save for service on the donor such service may be effected by pre-paid registered post to the usual or last known place of residence of the person to whom it is to be given or by personal service or in such other substituted manner as the Court may allow as being appropriate in the circumstances on an *ex parte* application for that purpose.

(4) The Court may, or where appropriate, the Registrar may in any case require such proof of service of the notice of the applicant's intention to seek the registration or of any other notice sent or purportedly sent to any person in any case in which it appears necessary to do so and may adjourn such application until such service or notification, as the case may be, has been proved to the satisfaction of the Court or the Registrar, as the case may be.

(5) In any case to which section 10(2) of the Act applies the Court may adjourn the application for registration until such enquiries as it makes or as it causes to be made are completed and may give such direction in relation to any enquiries which it thinks appropriate as appear necessary in the circumstances of the case.

(6) In any case in which a valid notice of objection to the registration has been given or for other sufficient reason the Court may require such party objecting

to the registration to file an affidavit or affidavits in support of the grounds of objection and the person concerned shall comply with the directions of the Court in relation to such matters. Notice of objection shall, as far as practicable, be in the Form No. 3 or No. 4 as the case may be.

(7) In any case in which it appears necessary in the interests of justice to the Court to do so, it may direct that an issue or issues arising in relation to an application for registration or an objection thereto be heard on oral evidence and may give such directions concerning the exchange of pleadings, or the making of discovery as appear necessary and proper in the circumstances of the case.

(8) In any case in which an objection to an attorney or to a power is established but an enduring power subsists as respects an attorney who is not affected thereby, the Court shall direct the registration of the enduring power of attorney by qualifying the registration by specifying in its order that the power concerned shall not be exercisable or shall be exercisable subject to conditions or, as the case may be, that the attorney concerned shall not exercise or purport to exercise the power originally intended to be granted and the power of attorney shall thereafter be subject to such qualification as is specified in the order.

Post Registration Applications

4.(1) Subsequent to the registration of an instrument an application:

(a) to disclaim a power pursuant to section 11(1)(b) of the Act, or

(b) for the exercise by the Court of any power conferred by section 12(2) to (6) inclusive of the Act;

shall be made by notice of motion to the Court and shall be lodged in the Office of the Wards of Court. Such motion shall as far as practicable be in the Form No. 2 as set out in the Appendix hereto and shall be grounded upon the affidavit of the moving party which shall fully set forth the facts and circumstances giving rise to the making of the application.

(2) The provisions of sub rules 2 to 9 inclusive of rule 3 shall apply *mutatis mutandis*, where applicable, in relation to any application brought under this rule.

The Registrar

5.(1) The Registrar shall keep and maintain a Register in which he shall register all instruments which are entitled to be registered as an enduring power of attorney under the provisions of the Act. Such Register shall record the date of application for registration, the date of registration, any qualification specified by the Court in relation to a registration and any applications with regard to the revocation or cancellation of the registration of an instrument.

(2) The Registrar shall maintain a cause book in which all applications made under the Act in relation to any enduring power of attorney (whether registered or unregistered) and the outcome of same shall be recorded. Such cause book shall only be available for inspection by the applicant, the donor, any person on whom a relevant notice has been served or such other person as the Registrar may, in his discretion, permit.

(3) The Registrar shall keep and retain in the Office of the Wards of Court

an attested copy of all enduring powers of attorney lodged with him for the purpose of registration or which are lodged in Court for the purposes of any application under the Act and shall supply attested copies to any person entitled to same pursuant to section 11 of the Act.

(4) The Registrar may, in any case in which it appears appropriate to do so, issue a certificate certifying that an application for registration has been made but not yet determined or that an application has been made which has resulted in the registration of the instrument to which it relates and such certificate may be given in the Form No. 5 in the Appendix hereto as may be appropriate.

Costs

6. The costs of any application to the Court or any objection to any application shall be in the discretion of the Court.

APPENDIX D

ENDURING POWERS OF ATTORNEY GUIDELINES FOR SOLICITORS*

An update to the Law Society's Guidelines for Solicitors in relation to Enduring Powers of Attorney (EPAs) created under the provisions of the Powers of Attorney Act 1996 (1996 Act) is now available.

The updated guidelines take account of developments in common law since the guidelines were last revised in 2009 and also has regard to the enactment of the Assisted Decision-Making (Capacity) Act 2015–see below.

By way of background, in 2004, the Law Society originally published Guidelines for Solicitors in relation to EPAs created under the provisions of the 1996 Act, with those guidelines being updated in 2009. In December 2015, the Assisted Decision-Making (Capacity) Act 2015 (2015 Act) was enacted with Part 7 of the Act dealing with EPAs. (Part 7 has not yet been commenced). The 2015 Act provides that, subject to certain exceptions, the 2015 Act will not apply to EPAs created under the 1996 Act. It also provides that from the date of the commencement of Part 7–a person shall not create an enduring power of attorney under the Act of 1996 and the Act of 1996 shall not apply to an enduring power of attorney created after that date (i.e. EPAs created under the 2015 Act). Therefore, until the commencement of the new provisions relating to EPAs, EPAs will continue to be created under the provisions of the 1996 Act and the 1996 Act will continue to apply to them even if they come into effect–ie are registered–after the commencement of the 2015 Act.

The Law Society has therefore decided to update the Guidelines for Solicitors in relation to EPAs being created under the provisions of the 1996 Act, to take account of developments in common law since the guidelines were updated in 2009 and also having regard to the enactment of the 2015 Act. Further Guidelines will be published in relation to EPAs to be created under the provisions of Part 7 of the 2015 Act when commenced.

1. Introduction

1.1. In 2004 the Law Society published Guidelines for Solicitors in relation to Enduring Powers of Attorney (EPAs) created under the provisions of the *Powers of Attorney Act 1996* (1996 Act), with those guidelines being updated in 2009.

1.2. In December 2015 the *Assisted Decision-Making (Capacity) Act 2015* (2015 Act) was enacted with Part 7 of the Act dealing with EPAs. (Part 7 has not yet been commenced.) The 2015 Act provides that subject to certain exceptions, the 2015 Act will not apply to EPAs created under the 1996 Act. It also provides that from the date of the commencement of Part 7–*a person shall not create an enduring power of attorney under the Act of 1996 and the Act of 1996 shall not apply to an enduring power of attorney created after that date* (i.e. EPAs created under the 2015 Act). Therefore, until the commencement of the new provisions relating to EPAs, EPAs will continue to be created under the provisions of the 1996 Act and the 1996 Act will continue to apply to them even if they come into effect – i.e. are registered–after the commencement of the 2015 Act.

1.3. The Law Society therefore decided to update the Guidelines for Solicitors in relation to EPAs being created under the provisions of the 1996 Act to take account of developments in common law since the guidelines were updated in 2009 and also having regard to the enactment of the 2015 Act. (Further Guidelines will be published in relation to EPAs to be created under the provisions of Part 7 of the 2015 Act when commenced.)

1.4. **The following points should be noted when advising a client creating an EPA under the 1996 Act:**

1.4.1. There is a presumption in common law (given statutory effect in the 2015 Act and will be a statutory presumption on the coming into force on the commencement of the 2015 Act) that every adult has the capacity to make a decision unless the contrary is clearly indicated. It must not be assumed that a *person lacks capacity to make a decision solely because of their age, disability, appearance, behaviour, medical condition (including intellectual disability, mental illness, dementia or scores on tests of cognitive function), their beliefs, their apparent inability to communicate, or the fact that they may make a decision that appears unwise.* (HSE National Consent Policy para 5.3.)

1.4.2. The decision of the High Court in *Fitzpatrick v K (No.2) [2008] IEHC* stated that decision-making capacity is to be defined on a functional or decision specific basis. Capacity is therefore to be assessed on the basis of a person's ability to understand the nature and consequences of a decision in the context of available choices at the time the decision has to be made. It is therefore not an across the board assessment of capacity but is issue specific and time specific. **It is important that the donor of an EPA fully understands the purport of creating an enduring power of attorney, intends the power to be effective only when the donor lacks decision-making capacity and the EPA is registered.**

1.4.3. Since the High Court's 2008 *Fitzpatrick* decision, the functional approach to the assessment of capacity is now contained in *HSE National Consent Policy* and the Medical Council's *Guide to Professional Conduct and Ethics for Registered Medical Practitioners* (7th edition 2009 and 8th edition 2016). The functional approach must therefore be used in the assessment of capacity to create an EPA. (The 2015 Act also gives statutory effect to the principle that decision-making capacity is to be construed functionally and will become a statutory obligation on the commencement of the 2015 Act.)

1.4.4. Best practice and to comply with international human rights standards requires that a person is supported and assisted to maximise his or her decision-making ability. (This current obligation is given statutory effect in the 2015 Act and will become a statutory obligation on the commencement of the 2015 Act.)

1.4.5. It is also current best practice to have regard to the Guiding Principles set out in S.8 of the *Assisted Decision-Making (Capacity) Act 2015*. Those principles (some of which already have statutory force in the 1996 Act) are extremely relevant once the EPA comes into effect – to include *the need to permit and encourage the donor to participate, or to improve the donor's ability to participate, as fully as possible in any decision affecting the donor.* (S.6 (7) 1996 Act.)

1.4.6. Ireland is due to ratify the *Hague Convention on the International Protection of Adults 2000* in 2016. Therefore an Irish EPA created under the 1996 Act may take effect in other jurisdictions but it is necessary to advise a client what jurisdictions come within the terms of the Hague Convention and also that the law applicable to **the manner of the exercise of an EPA is the law of the country where it is exercised.**

1.4.7. An EPA created under the 1996 Act can be revoked at any time while the donor has the decision-making capacity to do so and should the client wish. Once Part 7 of the 2015 Act is commenced the donor could revoke the EPA created under the 1996 Act and create an EPA under the 2015 Act. The solicitor should at this stage explain the reasons why a client might wish to do so. For example, there are annual reporting provisions contained in the 2015 Act. Also, at time of the registration of a 2015 EPA, the Director of the Decision Support Service is required to ascertain if the attorney/s appointed are suitable to carry out the functions of an attorney. These are possible safeguards that the client should be informed about. **It should be stressed to the client that once a 1996 Act EPA is created it will remain valid (unless amended or revoked) even after the commencement of the 2015 Act.**

1.4.8. Other legislation enacted since the 2009 Guidelines were published also need to be considered when advising a client with regard to the creation of an EPA under the 1996 Act. Examples: *Civil Partnership and Certain Rights and Obligations of Cohabitants Act 2010* and the *Personal Insolvency Act 2012.*

1.5. In advising clients with regard to the execution of an EPA, solicitors should note that different considerations apply in relation to donors who have full decision-making capacity and who wish to make provisions for a time when they may no longer have decision-making capacity and those donors whose decision-making capacity may be in question due to ill health or age and potentially are at a vulnerable stage but nevertheless have capacity to create an EPA but are more likely to be vulnerable to undue influence, fraud or exploitation.

2. Execution of Enduring Power of Attorney

2.1. Who is the client?

2.1.1. A solicitor should ensure that instructions are taken directly from the intending donor of an EPA. When written instructions are received from a client, a solicitor should arrange to meet the client personally and discuss the implications of, and advise the client with regard to, the execution of an EPA. When instructions are received from a third party for the preparation of an EPA, a solicitor should obtain instructions directly from the intending donor as to whether or not the intending donor wishes the solicitor to act for him/her. If such instructions are received, then the donor is your client and you must ensure that the donor is being fully and independently advised without regard to the interests of any third party and that the donor is not under pressure or being influenced to create an EPA.

2.1.2. A solicitor is obliged as part of the formal execution of an EPA to state that the solicitor is satisfied that the donor understood the effect of creating the enduring power and has no reason to believe that the instrument is being executed by the donor as a result of fraud or undue pressure. A solicitor should ensure that instructions are given freely by the client. (S.5 (2) 1996 Act.)

2.1.3. A solicitor should presume that the donor has the capacity to create an EPA unless the contrary is shown. If it is necessary to assess the donor's capacity to create an EPA then a functional assessment of capacity is required to comply with common law and in line with the national policy guidelines. (This obligation to construe decision-making capacity in a functional manner will become a statutory obligation when the 2015 Act is commenced.)

2.1.4. Part A of the EPA containing explanatory information is part of the EPA instrument and should not be detached from it. The intending donor should be advised to read Part A, or have it read to him/her and if necessary have the detail explained to him/her. However, the fact that Part A has been read by or to the intending donor does not relieve a solicitor of the obligation to interview the intending donor and make enquiries to satisfy the solicitor that the intending donor understands the effect of creating the EPA, intends the power to be effective only when the donor lacks decision-making capacity and once the EPA is registered.

2.2. Decision-making Capacity

2.2.1. It is important for a solicitor to explain fully the effect of creating the EPA and to ensure that the client understands this. By explaining the provisions in detail and questioning the client as to his/her wishes, it should be possible to ascertain whether or not the client understands the provisions of the EPA and that the client has the necessary decision-making ability to create an EPA. In the attendance note of the meeting with the client, a solicitor should record the client's understanding of the effect of creating the EPA. The scope and purpose of the power must be explained to the donor by the solicitor with a sufficient degree of clarity to ensure that the donor understands that the EPA creates a power of far-reaching effect. (See SCR [2015] IEHC 308.)

2.2.2. Understanding the effect of creating the EPA means the client must understand that he or she will effectively be passing over control of their assets to the attorney to take decisions with regard to those assets in the event that the donor lacks capacity to make decisions for him or herself at a later date and will be making critical decisions with regard to personal care. An EPA may also be created giving limited or simple authority to the attorney to do specified things on behalf of the donor and an EPA in this form may be more appropriate for a person whose decision-making capacity is limited but is able to make decisions about those specific issues.

2.2.3. Given that the assessment of decision-making capacity to create an EPA is a legal test and not a medical test, the obligation is for the solicitor to establish whether or not the client has the capacity to create an EPA.

2.3. Is an EPA appropriate?

2.3.1. A solicitor should advise the client, in addition to the benefits involved in the execution of an EPA, of the risks that, in the event the client lacks decision-making capacity, the attorney has control over the assets of the client and has the authority to make certain decisions on behalf of the client which may include care decisions which will affect the wellbeing of the donor.

2.3.2. Appropriate advice to the client includes advising the intending donor of the EPA of the alternative to having a registered power in place at the time they lack decision-making capacity, i.e. currently being made a Ward of Court and, on the commencement of the 2015 Act, of the alternative assisted decision-making mechanisms available.

2.3.3. An EPA may not be appropriate in the particular client's circumstances where:

- There have been persistent family disagreements, particularly if there is likely to be dispute between family members as to the management of assets and there is no alternative suitable person available for appointment. However, in certain circumstances the client may have specific wishes as to what is to happen in the event that he/she lacks decision-making capacity and perhaps an EPA limited to 'personal care' decisions may be appropriate. If this is the case, it should then be pointed out to the client that in the event of them lacking decision-making capacity it may be necessary for a court to appoint someone to make decisions on their behalf.
- The value of the client's assets is substantial and there is no person with the appropriate skills to manage the assets.

2.3.4. Solicitors should note that there is a **mandatory requirement** for a person entering into a debt settlement arrangement or a personal insolvency arrangement to make provision for the manner in which the debtor's debts are to be treated in the event that the debtor lacks decision-making capacity. (S.65 and S.99 *Personal Insolvency Act 2012*.) It is important to emphasise to the donor that the attorney to be appointed in such circumstances will have very clear obligations to fulfil in carrying out the debtor obligations under such an arrangement and therefore the appointment of an attorney with suitable skills to deal with such matters is essential.

2.4. Choice of Attorney

2.4.1. Although the choice of an attorney is a personal matter for the client, a solicitor should stress the need to appoint an attorney who is trustworthy and suitable to act as attorney. A solicitor should also advise the client that, in the event of the registration of the EPA, the attorney's actions will be subject to little or no supervision or reporting requirement under the 1996 Act. Solicitors should consider advising clients of the possibility that an additional 'condition' (as provided for in S.6 (2) of the 1996 Act) might be inserted into the EPA to specifically reference the fact that the donor wishes the attorneys to comply with the reporting obligations and provisions of the 2015 Act when commenced. (See S.75 of the 2015 Act.)

2.4.2. A solicitor should make enquiries about the client's choice of potential attorney in terms of the relationship with the client, suitability, trustworthiness, skills necessary to manage the client's financial affairs and empathy with the client's wishes with regard to his/her personal care decisions. A solicitor should also advise the client that a **conflict of interest** may arise for an attorney, for example, where the attorney has an interest in property owned by the client (i.e. shareholder in the same company or co-owner of property) or is a potential beneficiary in the donor's estate. If there is potential for such conflict of interest the client should be advised of the option to create the EPA with 'conditions and restrictions' which could deal with such a potential problem. (S.6 of the 1996 Act.)

2.4.3. The issue as to whether the client should appoint joint attorneys should include advice on the greater opportunity for abuse which the appointment of a sole attorney provides. The solicitor should explain that the donor has the option, when appointing more than one attorney, to specify whether the attorneys are to be permitted to act jointly or jointly and severally, i.e. whether they must act together when making decisions.

2.4.4. In such circumstances clients should be advised of the implications of S.14(3) of the 1996 Act which provides:

> "*where two or more persons are appointed (or are deemed to be appointed) to act jointly as Attorneys, then, in the case of the death, lack of capacity or disqualification of any one or more of them, the remaining Attorney or Attorneys may continue to act, whether solely or jointly, as the case may be, unless the instrument creating the power expressly provides to the contrary.*"

2.4.5. A solicitor should take clear instructions as to whether the client wishes to appoint joint attorneys or whether the client wishes to appoint a sole attorney or joint attorneys with substitute attorneys. Any provision for substitute attorney must be made at the time of execution of the EPA.

2.5. Notice Parties

2.5.1. Notice of the execution of an EPA is required to be given to at least two persons. It is important that a solicitor advises the client carefully of the order of persons who must be notified, which are clearly set out in paragraph 7 of the Enduring Powers of Attorney Regulations 1996 (SI 196 of 1996).

2.5.2. The donor must give notice of the execution of the EPA as soon as practicable to at least two persons. None of them may be an attorney under the power. At least one must be:

i. The donor's spouse/civil partner, if living with the donor, or
ii. If (i) does not apply (if the donor is unmarried, widowed or separated), notification must be given to a child of the donor (if applicable), or
iii. If (i) and (ii) do not apply, to any relative (that is, parent, sibling, grandchild, widow(er) of a child, nephew or niece, in that order.

2.5.3. Where a spouse/civil partner is appointed as attorney, the spouse/civil partner may not also be a notice party and the donor should notify a child, or other relative if there are no children or the child/children are also appointed as attorneys under the instrument.

2.5.4. There is no period of notice prescribed by the legislation but the notice should be served by registered or recorded post as soon as practicable (preferably within 30 days) of the execution of the EPA and affidavits of service sworn. Care should be taken to safely retain the documentary evidence of posting, as this will be the subject of an averment–perhaps many years later–in the affidavit grounding the application to register the EPA.

2.6. Scope of Authority

2.6.1. **Business and financial affairs**

The solicitor should advise the client of the meaning of giving a general authority or a limited power to the attorney. The type of restrictions that are possible in an EPA should be explained to the client. For example, a restriction that the attorney may not sell the donor's house. A solicitor should then obtain clear instructions as to whether the authority to be given is with regard to all, or only specified assets, of the client. If the client wishes the authority to be subject to restrictions and conditions, then careful drafting is required. A solicitor should point out to the client that, if assets are sold by their attorneys after the EPA has been registered, this may have implications for specific bequests contained in a Will. The client should therefore be encouraged to review a Will at the time of the execution of an EPA.

If the EPA is being executed with limitations a solicitor should advise the client of the consequences of that–it may be necessary to have the client taken into Wardship (or if registered after the commencement of the 2015 Act to have the court appoint a decision-making representative) should it become necessary to make a decision/s for which authority is not given in the EPA.

The solicitor should ascertain if the client owns any property jointly with others and, if so, to ascertain:

- Does a presumption of a resulting trust arise?
- Does the presumption of advancement arise?
- Was there an intention to benefit the joint owner, either at the date of transfer or at the date of death?
- Details of the client's investments should be ascertained and the client's wishes with regard to investments should also be ascertained and discussed.

2.6.2. **Personal Care Decisions**

A solicitor should advise the client of the possibility of granting powers over personal care decisions and ascertain if the client wishes anyone other than the attorney to be consulted with regard to such decisions.

A solicitor should also enquire as to whether or not the client has separately executed any form of **advance healthcare directive** with regard to the refusal of or consent to medical treatment. The client should be advised to inform the attorney of such directive.

Where it is intended to grant powers over personal care decisions to the attorney, a solicitor should draw the attention of the donor to the categories of personal care decisions in respect of which an attorney may be given authority and delete any which the intending donor does not wish to grant. (Note that personal care decisions under the 1996 Act do not extend to healthcare decisions).

The costs of long-term care should be discussed with the client and their wishes with regard to care at home or in an alternative facility should be noted.

The conferring of personal care decisions **does not give the attorney any authority** to detain or restrain the donor.

In preparing the statutory form for an EPA, a solicitor should ensure the correct schedule is being completed. The form set out in the first schedule is appropriate when general authority is being completed and it includes personal care decisions. The form in the second schedule should only be used if the authority being given is restricted to personal-care decisions only.

2.7. Gifts and Remuneration

2.7.1. A donor of an EPA can specifically provide that an attorney has the authority to make gifts of the donor's assets when the EPA takes effect.

2.7.2. As the provision for making gifts is open to abuse, a solicitor should advise the client of S.6 (5) of the 1996 Act which limits the making of:

> *"gifts of a seasonal nature or at a time, or on an anniversary, or a birth or marriage, to persons (including the attorney) who are related to or connected with the donor and gifts to any charity to which the donor made or might be expected to make gifts, provided the value of each such gift is not unreasonable, having regard to all the circumstances and in particular, the extent of the donor's assets."*

2.7.3. In the case of provision for remunerating the attorney, clear instructions should be obtained from the client as to the circumstances in which remuneration should be paid. A solicitor should discuss with the client whether it is necessary to provide for the payment of remuneration at all. In cases where a professional advisor is being appointed, a charging clause should be included. (See 2.8 below).

2.8. Solicitor – Attorney

2.8.1. When a solicitor is being appointed an attorney, the client should be advised that there will be a professional charge for acting and the client approval should be obtained for the making of such charges. For the avoidance of doubt, if a solicitor is being appointed an attorney, then a charging clause should be included in the EPA. A solicitor should also advise the client that, in the event of the registration of the EPA, provision should be made for the solicitor's professional fees to be approved by an independent third party. A solicitor who is appointed as an attorney should not sign the prescribed certificate. (*A potential conflict of interest may arise where a solicitor is being appointed, particularly as sole attorney. It is best to avoid any circumstances where such an issue can be raised*).

2.8.2. For the avoidance of doubt, a partner or a colleague in the same firm may sign the certificate.

2.8.3. A solicitor who is being appointed attorney in their professional capacity should consider their professional indemnity insurance and how matters will be dealt with on retirement from practice.

2.9. Order of Execution

2.9.1. After the donor has signed the EPA, then the attorney(s) should sign and then the doctor. The solicitor should ensure that the registered medical practitioner is aware of the form of statement required by him or her. It should state:

> "***That in his or her opinion at the time the EPA was executed, the donor had the mental capacity, with the assistance of such explanations as may have been given to the donor, to understand the effect of creating the EPA.***" (S.5(2) 1996 Act.)

2.9.2. When the instrument has been completed, a solicitor should ensure that it is properly executed in accordance with the 1996 Act and should discuss with the client where the original of the instrument should be kept.

2.10. Revocation before Registration

A solicitor should advise the client that he/she can revoke an EPA at any time before it is registered. The form of revocation (which need not be by deed) should specifically identify the EPA being revoked. The original EPA or a copy thereof should be exhibited in the revocation.

Notice of revocation should be served on the named attorney(s). As a matter of prudence, and in order to avoid difficulties at a later stage, the formalities that apply to the execution of an EPA should be complied with–that is notice should be served on the notice parties and a solicitor's statement should confirm that the client understands the effect of revocation, and a registered medical practitioner should state that the donor had the necessary mental capacity (with such explanations that may have been given to the donor) to understand the effect of revocation. A functional approach to capacity is required to comply with common law and in line with national policy guidelines.

Once the EPA is registered a court application is necessary to effect any revocation or cancellation of the registration. A solicitor should advise the client of the effect of registration and in particular the provision of S.11 (1)(c) which includes a restriction on the donor to extend or restrict the scope of the authority given in the EPA.

2.11. Disclaimer by attorney prior to registration

No disclaimer, whether by deed or otherwise, of an EPA that has not been registered shall be valid unless and until the attorney gives notice of it to the donor.

2.12. Invalidation of an EPA

See the provisions of S.5 (6), (7) (8) and (9) of the 1996 Act, as amended by S.50 (a) of the *Family Law (Divorce) Act 1996* and S.104 of the *Civil Partnership and Certain Rights and Obligations of Cohabitants Act 2010* for the circumstances in which an EPA shall be invalidated.

2.13. Storage of Documents

If the client is not retaining the original documents personally, a solicitor should ensure that the original EPA together with relevant certificates, copy of notices to notice parties, and evidence of service of notices should be stored safely.

3. Prior to registration

3.1. Jurisdiction of the Court

On application by any interested party, and whether or not the attorney has made application for registration of the EPA, the High Court may exercise any power with respect to the EPA, or to the attorney appointed to act under it if the Court is of the opinion that it is necessary. This could apply where, for example, the attorney has not taken steps to register the EPA. (S.8 1996 Act.)

3.2. Substitute Attorney

Where a named attorney has died or disclaimed the EPA, evidence of death or disclaimer must be produced to the Registrar Wards of Court to enable registration of the EPA with the substitute attorney.

3.3. Validity of EPA

If there is any question as to the validity of the EPA prior to registration, then an application may be made by the attorney to the High Court for its determination. (S.9 (3) 1996 Act.)

3.4. Defective EPA

Where the EPA differs in an immaterial respect, in form or mode of expression, from the form prescribed in the regulations, the Registrar Wards of Court may register the EPA. Notwithstanding that the EPA does not comply with the legislative provisions, the High Court may admit the EPA for registration. (S.10 (5) 1996 Act.)

3.5. Foreign EPAs

There have been instances where EPAs under the legislation of England and Wales have been admitted for registration under S.10 (5) of the 1996 Act. (See Practice Direction of the Wards of Court Office on website at http://www.courts.ie and Introduction above for comments on the impact of Ireland ratifying the Hague Convention.)

4. Registration of EPA.

Prior to, and on the registration of an EPA, instructions may be accepted from an attorney, but a solicitor continues to owe a duty to the client (donor of the EPA).

4.1. Role and Obligation of Attorneys

A solicitor should advise the attorney of his/her role and obligation to the donor and, in particular, should deal specifically with the following points:

4.1.1. The circumstances in which a person is disqualified from acting as an attorney or the circumstances when a person may be considered unsuitable to act as an attorney. It should be explained to the client that, in certain circumstances, a person will be disqualified from acting as an attorney – for example, where the attorney is a spouse/civil partner/cohabitant and there has been a subsequent annulment or dissolution of marriage or dissolution of the civil partnership or an ending of the cohabitant arrangement, disqualification under the Companies Acts or a connection with the nursing home in which the donor resides. (See S.5 (4) and (7) of the 1996 Act as amended by the S.50 of the *Family Law (Divorce) Act, 1996*.)

4.1.2. S.5 (4) of the 1996 Act provides that a person who has been adjudicated bankrupt will also be disqualified from being appointed as attorney. Prudence would indicate that disqualification would also extend to a person who had entered into a debt settlement arrangement or a personal insolvency arrangement following the enactment of the Personal Insolvency Act 2012.

4.1.3. The attorney should also consider his/her suitability in the context of conflicts of interest, both present and future.

4.1.4. The scope of the authority given in the EPA and the fact that the EPA does not come into force until it has been registered, but that the attorney may take certain actions/make decisions pending registration if an application for registration has been made and the donor does not have the decision making capacity to make the relevant decision or take the relevant action. (S.7 (2) of the 1996 Act.) In determining whether the donor has decision-making capacity to make a relevant decision, a functional approach to capacity is required to comply with common law and in line with national policy guidelines.

4.1.5. If the scope of the authority includes personal-care decisions, advise what decisions can be made, and whether the EPA provides that any other party be consulted.

4.1.6. There is a statutory requirement on the attorney under the 1996 Act to act 'in the best interests' of the donor in making personal care decisions. The concept of best interest also involves considering whether there is an alternative method of obtaining the same result, which would be less restrictive of the donor's freedom of action. (S.6 (7) of the 1996 Act.) This statutory requirement **includes having regard to the past and present wishes and feelings of the donor** and the factors which the donor would consider if he or she were able to do so and the need to permit and **encourage the donor to participate or to improve the donor's ability to participate as fully as possible in any decision**, and consulting with persons caring for the donor or interested in the donor's welfare. Best practice and compliance with international human rights standards requires a person to be supported and assisted to maximise his or her decision-making capacity.

4.1.7. Where the scope of the authority permits the attorney to decide where the donor may live, the attorney should ascertain whether the donor has the relevant decision-making capacity to decide where he or she wishes to live and if so implement or assist with implementation of those wishes. In the absence of the relevant decision-making capacity the solicitor should advise the attorney of the significance, both legally and for the donor, of considering whether the donor should change residence from their home to a care facility, including the need for the attorney to seek relevant medical and legal advice (and to consult with named individuals, discussed below).

4.1.8. If the EPA created by the donor extends to the compliance by the donor with his/her mandatory requirements of entering into a debt settlement or personal insolvency arrangement then the attorney needs to be advised of the obligations of the donor under any such arrangement. (See S.65 and S.99 *Personal Insolvency Act 2012.*)

4.1.9. The requirement to keep accounts of the donor's property and affairs and, if required, to produce the accounting records to the High Court. The current best practice is for the records of the attorney to include proper annual accounts and financial records in relation to the donor's income and expenditure and to include an annual account in writing of the performance of functions by the attorney. The accounts should also include details of all costs, expenses and remuneration paid to and claimed by the attorney on an annual basis.

4.1.10. The requirement, if applicable, to make tax returns in respect of income and capital gains to the Revenue Commissioners on behalf of the donor.

4.1.11. The requirement to keep the donor's property separate from the attorney's property – an attorney is simply an agent of the donor. (The registration of the EPA should be noted on the accounts of the donor held by financial institutions, and the proceeds of the accounts should not be transferred into the name of the attorney.)

4.1.12. The requirement in relation to the separation of funds may not be required depending on all the circumstances where funds are held jointly for spouses/civil partner and one of the spouses/civil partner is the donor and the other spouse/civil partner is the sole attorney.

4.1.13. The requirement not to profit from position as an attorney.

4.1.14. If relevant, the requirement to consult with named individuals. (Even if not required by the EPA to consult with named individuals, a solicitor should advise an attorney that it is prudent to keep family members generally informed of transactions in relation to the donor's assets on an annual basis).

4.1.15. The provisions in the EPA and the legislation in relation to gifts. (See 2.7 above.)

4.1.16. The provisions in the EPA and legislation in relation to expenses incurred by attorney(s) and remuneration of attorneys.

4.1.17. The provisions in the legislation and the EPA in relation to the use of the donor's assets for the benefit of others (including the attorney) and the limitations of this power. (S.6(4) of the 1996 Act.)

4.1.18. The fact that the attorney is an agent of the donor and that the attorney must use proper care in exercising the authority under the EPA. It is important that the attorney understands that the scope of his/her authority is limited to the authority set out in the EPA and as provided for by the legislation.

4.1.19. The fact that the attorney may disclaim at any time up to registration of the EPA, and thereafter only on notice to the donor and with the consent of the High Court.

4.1.20. The attorney should also be advised that the High Court has extensive functions with regard to registered EPAs, which includes power to cancel the registration of an EPA. (See generally S.12 of the 1996 Act.)

4.1.21. The attorney should be advised if any conditions or restrictions are set out in the EPA by which he/she is to exercise the authority given to attorney in the EPA – for example is there a condition that the attorney must file annual reports to the Director of the Decision Support Service when the 2015 Act has commenced?

If a solicitor suspects that an attorney may be misusing an EPA or acting dishonestly, he/she should notify the Registrar of the Wards of Court Office.

The High Court may cancel the registration of an instrument – for example on being satisfied that having regard to all the circumstances, the attorney is unsuitable to be the donor's attorney; on being satisfied that fraud or undue pressure was used to induce the donor to create the power. In the case of theft or fraud, the Gardaí should be notified.

4.2. Application for Registration

4.2.1. A solicitor, on receiving instructions to register an EPA, should personally satisfy him/herself that the donor is, or is becoming, incapable of managing his/her affairs understanding that the assessment is a legal test and not a medical test. The solicitor should ensure that in making this assessment the donor's capacity is construed functionally as is required in common law and in line with national policy guidelines.

4.2.2. The following steps should be taken in registering an EPA:

(i) Obtain a medical certificate from a registered medical practitioner to the effect that the donor is, or where appropriate, is becoming incapable, by reason of a mental condition, of managing and administering his/her own property and affairs. The solicitor should write to the registered medical practitioner explaining the necessity to consider the issues from a functional perspective making reference to the common law assessment of capacity and the national policy guidelines. (In particular the registered medical practitioner should be referred to the Medical Council's *Guide to Professional Conduct and Ethics for Registered Medical Practitioners* 8th edition 2016.)

(ii) Arrange with the attorney(s) to sign the following forms of notice of intention to apply for registration (a separate form is signed in respect of each notice party):

a) Notice of intention to apply for registration addressed to the donor,

b) Notice of intention to apply for registration addressed to the notice parties (note part 1, first schedule to the 1996 Act as to the order of precedence of entitlement to notice of intention to apply, where notice parties are deceased or otherwise),

c) Notice of intention to apply for registration addressed to Registrar Wards of Court.

(iii) Serve the donor by registered post with the notice as indicated at (ii)(a) above, i.e. notice of intention to apply for registration.

(iv) Have an affidavit of service in connection with serving the notice of intention to apply for registration on the donor sworn.

(v) Serve the notice parties by registered post with the notice as indicated at (ii)(b) above, i.e., notice of intention to apply for registration.

(vi) Have affidavits of service in connection with serving the notice of intention to apply for registration on the notice parties sworn.

(vii) Serve notice (by ordinary post) on Registrar of the Wards of Court of the intention to apply for registration.

(viii) Wait for five-week notice period to expire.

(ix) Arrange for the attorney(s) to swear an affidavit grounding the application for registration, setting forth fully the facts and/or circumstances giving rise to the application.

(x) File the following documentation (together with affidavits of service at (xii) below) with the Registrar of the Wards of Court Office:

a) Application for registration of EPA (see form no 1 in the appendix to order 129, rule 3, Rules of Superior Courts 1986),

b) Original EPA,

c) Copy notice of execution by the donor of the EPA given to the notice parties at the time of the execution of the EPA,

d) Copy notice of intention to apply for registration given to the donor,

e) Copy notice of intention to apply for registration given to the notice parties,

f) Affidavit of service in relation to the service on the notice parties of the notice of execution,

g) Affidavit of service in relation to the service on the donor of the notice of intention to apply for registration,

h) Affidavit of service in relation to service on the notice parties of the notice of intention to apply for registration,

i) Medical certificate from a registered medical practitioner,

j) Affidavit sworn by attorney(s), at (ix) above.

(xi) a) A copy of this application for registration should be personally served on the donor, and

b) A copy of this application for registration should be served on the notice parties by registered post.

(xii) a) Swear affidavit of service of application for registration on donor,

b) Swear affidavit of service of application for registration on notice parties.

5. Post Registration Matters

5.1. Notification to the Registrar Wards of Court after registration and when the EPA has come into effect

The attorney should be advised to notify the Registrar Wards of Court if any of the following events occur post registration:

- Change of address of attorney.
- Change of address of donor.
- Death of donor.
- Where the attorney no longer has capacity to carry out his/her functions as attorney, then notification of this should be made by their attorney/committee or decision-making representative (if applicable).
- Where the attorney dies their personal representative should make the notification.
- Any other event which would terminate or invalidate the EPA, for example, if the donor recovers decision-making capacity, or if the attorney is adjudicated a bankrupt. It would also be prudent to notify the Registrar if the attorney enters into a debt settlement arrangement or a personal insolvency arrangement.

5.2. Revocation by donor of EPA

A revocation post registration of an EPA by a donor is not valid unless and until the court confirms the revocation. The application must be on notice to the attorney(s) (Ss.11 (1) (a) and 12(3) of the 1996 Act).

5.3. Disclaimer/resignation by attorney

5.3.1. The attorney should be advised that, in the event of the attorney wishing to disclaim/resign as attorney post registration of the EPA, he/she may only do so with the consent of the court upon application made on notice to the donor (S.11 (1) (b) 1996 Act).

5.3.2. If there is a joint attorney and the authority provides for several liability, then the continuing attorney will be in a position to continue to act. Likewise, if the EPA provides for a substitute attorney and the substitute attorney is willing to act, then the resignation will be effective.

5.4. Assets of the donor

The attorney should be advised of the following regarding the assets of the donor:

- To prepare a full inventory of assets to act as a checklist if any disputes arise in the future.

- The donor's money and property remain the property of the donor and should stay in the donor's name. The attorney has authority to deal with the property and assets but not to transfer/convert them into the ownership of the attorney.
- On no account should the money of the donor be intermingled with that of the attorney, save that if the attorney is a person who habitually held money in joint names with the donor (for example a spouse/civil partner) then that can continue.
- Keep full accounts for production if necessary to the High Court.

5.5. Complaints about an attorney

5.5.1. The attorney should be advised that the provisions of the 2015 Act (once commenced) regarding complaints about an attorney apply whether the EPA is signed and/or registered before or after the coming into force of the 2015 Act (S.76 (2) of 2015 Act). In other words EPAs created under the 1996 Act will come within the complaints provisions of the 2015 Act when the 2015 Act is commenced. This provides that **any person** (or the Director of the Decision Support Service on his/her own initiative) can make a complaint that

- An attorney is acting outside the scope of the powers given by the donor.
- That an attorney is unable to perform the duties or obligations imposed by the EPA.
- That fraud, coercion or undue pressure was exercised to force the donor to sign the EPA.

5.5.2. The Director of the Decision Support Service has power to fully investigate the complaint and, if the complaint is upheld, can make an application to the Circuit Court for a direction, including a direction that the attorney be removed as attorney.

5.6. Termination of EPA

The attorney should be advised that the functions of an attorney cease immediately on the death of the donor of the EPA.

Where the court cancels the registration of an EPA, it shall by order revoke the EPA (S.12 (5) of the 1996 Act).

PART 2

ASSISTED DECISION-MAKING (CAPACITY) ACT 2015

PART 2

ASSISTED DECISION-MAKING (CAPACITY) ACT 2015

This Part contains the provisions of Pts 7 and 11 of the Assisted Decision-Making (Capacity) Act 2015 (the "2015 Act") which, as of the date of publication, has not yet been commenced. It refers only to Enduring Powers of Attorney created after such commencement. This Act was signed by the President on the 30 December 2015. This Part also contains certain sections, including certain definition sections, from the 2015 Act which are referred to in Pt 7.

It was envisaged, when the Bill was published in July 2013, that the Act would apply to Enduring Powers created under Pt II of the Powers of Attorney Act 1996 (the "1996 Act") where the instrument creating the power had not been registered under s.10 of the 1996 Act before the commencement of the relevant section. However, this was reconsidered, and the following statement was made by Minister of State at the Department of Health, Kathleen Lynch on 9 December 2015 in *Seanad Éireann*:

> "One of the main substantive changes to Part 7 is that the director will not register enduring powers which have been created under the 1996 Act but have yet to be registered. I have received legal advice stating it would not be possible for the director to register these enduring powers under this Bill. They will have to be registered under the 1996 Act by the Office of the Wards of Court, which is the current system. However, the attorneys appointed under these enduring powers and all other powers registered under the 1996 Act will be subject to the new complaints and offences provision I am proposing to insert by way of amendments Nos. 188 and 192. I believe the number of executed but not yet registered enduring powers under the 1996 Act will be small."

The Part of the 2015 Act dealing with Enduring Powers was largely untouched from the date the Bill was published until Committee Stage at the Seanad, wherein all sections of the Bill dealing with Enduring Powers of Attorney were deleted and replaced with new sections which "align the provisions with the UN Convention of Rights of Persons with Disabilities and current international best practise"(244(6) *Seanad Éireann Debates* 9 December 2015). The new sections relating to enduring powers refer to provisions set out in earlier sections of the Act. Several definitions relevant to Pt 7 are contained in earlier sections of the Act, and are reproduced at the outset of this Part.

TABLE OF CERTAIN DEFINITIONS REFERRED TO IN PT 7 OF THE 2015 ACT

Section 2—(Designated Centre) "Designated Centre" has the meaning it has in section 2 of the Health Act 2007.
Section 2—(Relevant Person) "relevant person" means— (a) a person whose capacity is in question or may shortly be in question in respect of one or more than one matter, (b) a person who lacks capacity in respect of one or more than one matter, or (c) a person who falls within paragraphs (a) and (b) at the same time but in respect of different matters, as the case requires.
Section 2—(Healthcare Professional) "Healthcare Professional" means a member of any health or social care profession whether or not the profession is a designated profession within the meaning of section 3 of the Health and Social Care Profession Act 2005.
Section 2—(Customary Occasions) "Customary Occasions" means— (a) The occasion or anniversary of a birth, marriage or civil partnership, or (b) Any other occasion on which gifts are customarily made within families or among friends or associates.
Section 2—(Personal Welfare) "personal welfare", in relation to a relevant person, means one or more of the following matters: (a) accommodation, including whether or not the relevant person should live in a designated centre; (b) participation by the relevant person in employment, education or training; (c) participation by the relevant person in social activities; (d) decisions on any social services provided or to be provided to the relevant person; (e) healthcare; (f) other matters relating to the relevant person's well-being;
Section 2—(Property and Affairs) "property and affairs", in relation to a relevant person, means one or more of the following matters: (a) the custody, control and management of some or all of the relevant person's property or property rights;

(b) the sale, exchange, mortgaging, charging, gift or other disposition of the relevant person's property;
(c) the acquisition of property by the relevant person, or on his or her behalf;
(d) the carrying on, on behalf of the relevant person, of any profession, trade or business which may lawfully be carried on by a person other than the relevant person;
(e) the making of a decision which will have the effect of dissolving a partnership in which the relevant person is a partner;
(f) the carrying out of any contract entered into by the relevant person;
(g) the discharge of the relevant person's debts, tax and duty liabilities and obligations or other obligations;
(h) the execution or exercise of any of the powers or discretions vested in the relevant person as a tenant for life;
(i) providing, to the extent that the relevant person might have been expected to do so, for the needs of a decision-making assistant, a co-decision-maker, an attorney, a designated healthcare representative or a decision-making representative for the relevant person or of other persons;
(j) the conduct of proceedings before any court or tribunal, whether in the name of the relevant person or on his or her behalf;
(k) making an application for housing, social welfare or other benefits or otherwise protecting or advancing the interests of the relevant person in relation to those matters.

Section 2—(Relevant Decision)

"relevant decision"—

(a) in relation to a decision made, or to be made, by a decision-making assistant appointer with the assistance of a decision-making assistant for that appointer, means a decision on a matter the subject of the decision-making assistance agreement which appointed that decision-making assistant and which falls within the scope of that agreement,
(b) in relation to a decision made, or to be made, jointly by a co-decision-maker appointer and a co-decision-maker for that appointer, means a decision on a matter the subject of the co-decision-making agreement which appointed that co-decision-maker and which falls within the scope of that agreement,
(c) in relation to a decision made, or to be made, by a court on behalf of a relevant person, means a decision on a matter the subject of the decision-making order and which falls within the scope of that order,
(d) in relation to a decision made, or to be made, by a decision-making representative on behalf of a relevant person, means a decision on a matter the subject of the decision-making representation order which appointed that decision-making representative and which falls within the scope of that order,

(e) in relation to a decision made, or to be made, by an attorney on behalf of a relevant person, means a decision on a matter the subject of the enduring power of attorney which appointed that attorney and which falls within the scope of that power, and

(f) in relation to a decision made, or to be made, under an advance healthcare directive (and whether or not there is a designated healthcare representative under the directive), means a decision which falls within the scope of that directive.

Section 3—(Capacity)

3(1) Subject to subsections (2) to (6), for the purposes of this Act, a person's capacity shall be assessed on the basis of his or her ability to understand, at the time that a decision is to be made, the nature and consequence of the decision to be made by him or her in the context of the available choices at that time.

(2) A person lacks the capacity to make a decision if he or she is unable—

(a) to understand the information relevant to the decision,

(b) to retain that information long enough to make a voluntary choice,

(c) to use or weigh that information as part of the process of making the decision, or

(d) to communicate his or her decision (whether by talking, writing, using sign language, assistive technology, or any other means) or, if the implementation of the decision requires the act of a third party, to communicate by any means with that third party.

(3) A person is not to be regarded as unable to understand the information relevant to a decision if he or she is able to understand an explanation of it given to him or her in a way that is appropriate to his or her circumstances (whether using clear language, visual aids or any other means).

(4) The fact that a person is able to retain the information relevant to a decision for a short period only does not prevent him or her from being regarded as having the capacity to make the decision.

(5) The fact that a person lacks capacity in respect of a decision on a particular matter at a particular time does not prevent him or her from being regarded as having capacity to make decisions on the same matter at another time.

(6) The fact that a person lacks capacity in respect of a decision on a particular matter does not prevent him or her from being regarded as having capacity to make decisions on other matters.

(7) For the purposes of this section, information relevant to a decision shall be construed as including information about the reasonably foreseeable consequences of—

(a) each of the available choices at the time the decision is made, or

(b) failing to make the decision.

Section 4—(Courts)

(1) Subject to subsection (3), sections 37, 85 (6)(b) and 89 (2), Parts 6, 10 and 11, the Circuit Court shall have exclusive jurisdiction under this Act and the performance of the functions of that court conferred by this section shall be within the jurisdiction of the circuit of the Circuit Court and such jurisdiction shall be exercised by the circuit of the Circuit Court in which—

(a) the relevant person the subject of an application under this Act is residing or carrying on business at the time the application is made, or

(b) the relevant person the subject of an application under this Act has resided at any time during the period of 3 years immediately prior to the making of the application.

(2) An application to the Circuit Court under this Act may be made—

(a) in such office of, or attached to, the Circuit Court within the circuit concerned,

(b) in such combined court office (within the meaning of section 14 of the Courts and Court Officers Act 2009) within the circuit concerned, or

(c) in such office of the Courts Service, within the circuit concerned, designated by the Courts Service for the purpose of this Act,

as may be prescribed by rules of court.

(3) Notwithstanding any other provision of this Act—

(a) any decision regarding the donation of an organ from a living donor shall, where the donor is a person who lacks capacity, be determined by the High Court, and

(b) where an application in connection with the withdrawal of life-sustaining treatment from a person who lacks capacity comes before the courts for adjudication, that application shall be heard by the High Court.

(4) Nothing in this Act shall be construed as authorising any person to give consent for a non-therapeutic sterilisation procedure to be carried out on a person who lacks capacity.

Section 8—(Guiding Principles)

8. (1) The principles set out in subsections (2) to (10) shall apply for the purposes of an intervention in respect of a relevant person, and the intervener shall give effect to those principles accordingly.

(2) It shall be presumed that a relevant person who falls within paragraph (a) of the definition of "relevant person" in section 2(1) has capacity in respect of the matter concerned unless the contrary is shown in accordance with the provisions of this Act.

(3) A relevant person who falls within paragraph (a) of the definition of "relevant person" in section 2 (1) shall not be considered as unable to make a decision in respect of the matter concerned unless all practicable steps have been taken, without success, to help him or her to do so.

(4) A relevant person who falls within paragraph (a) of the definition of "relevant person" in section 2 (1) shall not be considered as unable to make a decision in respect of the matter concerned merely by reason of making, having made, or being likely to make, an unwise decision.

(5) There shall be no intervention in respect of a relevant person unless it is necessary to do so having regard to the individual circumstances of the relevant person.

(6) An intervention in respect of a relevant person shall—

(a) be made in a manner that minimises—

(i) the restriction of the relevant person's rights, and

(ii) the restriction of the relevant person's freedom of action,

(b) have due regard to the need to respect the right of the relevant person to dignity, bodily integrity, privacy, autonomy and control over his or her financial affairs and property,

(c) be proportionate to the significance and urgency of the matter the subject of the intervention, and

(d) be as limited in duration in so far as is practicable after taking into account the particular circumstances of the matter the subject of the intervention.

(7) The intervener, in making an intervention in respect of a relevant person, shall—

(a) permit, encourage and facilitate, in so far as is practicable, the relevant person to participate, or to improve his or her ability to participate, as fully as possible, in the intervention,

(b) give effect, in so far as is practicable, to the past and present will and preferences of the relevant person, in so far as that will and those preferences are reasonably ascertainable,

(c) take into account—

(i) the beliefs and values of the relevant person (in particular those expressed in writing), in so far as those beliefs and values are reasonably ascertainable, and

(ii) any other factors which the relevant person would be likely to consider if he or she were able to do so, in so far as those other factors are reasonably ascertainable,

(d) unless the intervener reasonably considers that it is not appropriate or practicable to do so, consider the views of—

(i) any person named by the relevant person as a person to be consulted on the matter concerned or any similar matter, and

(ii) any decision-making assistant, co-decision-maker, decision-making representative or attorney for the relevant person,

(e) act at all times in good faith and for the benefit of the relevant person, and

(f) consider all other circumstances of which he or she is aware and which it would be reasonable to regard as relevant.

(8) The intervener, in making an intervention in respect of a relevant person, may consider the views of—

(a) any person engaged in caring for the relevant person,

(b) any person who has a bona fide interest in the welfare of the relevant person, or

(c) healthcare professionals.

(9) In the case of an intervention in respect of a person who lacks capacity, regard shall be had to—

(a) the likelihood of the recovery of the relevant person's capacity in respect of the matter concerned, and

(b) the urgency of making the intervention prior to such recovery.

(10) The intervener, in making an intervention in respect of a relevant person—

(a) shall not attempt to obtain relevant information that is not reasonably required for making a relevant decision,

(b) shall not use relevant information for a purpose other than in relation to a relevant decision, and

(c) shall take reasonable steps to ensure that relevant information—

(i) is kept secure from unauthorised access, use or disclosure, and

(ii) is safely disposed of when he or she believes it is no longer required.

Section 94—(Appointment of Director)

94. (1) The Mental Health Commission shall appoint a person to be known as the Director of the Decision Support Service to perform the functions conferred on the Director by this Act.

(2) The Director shall—

(a) be appointed by the Mental Health Commission on the recommendation of the Public Appointments Service after a competition for that purpose under section 47 of the Public Service Management (Recruitment and Appointments) Act 2004 has been held, and

(b) have the appropriate experience, qualifications, training and expertise to enable him or her to efficiently and effectively perform the functions conferred on him or her.

(3) A person is not eligible for appointment as the Director if he or she—

(a) is a member of either House of the Oireachtas,

(b) is entitled under the rules of procedure of the European Parliament to sit in that Parliament, or

(c) is a member of a local authority within the meaning of the Local Government Act 2001.

Section 99—(Special visitors and general visitors)

(1) The Director may, in accordance with this section, appoint a person to be a special visitor or general visitor.

(2) A special visitor—

(a) is a registered medical practitioner who has particular knowledge, expertise and experience as respects the capacity of persons, or

(b) is a person who, although not a registered medical practitioner, is, in the opinion of the Director, a person who has particular knowledge, expertise and experience as respects the capacity of persons.

(3) A general visitor is a person who, in the opinion of the Director, is a person who possesses relevant qualifications, or has other relevant expertise or experience, to assist the Director in performing his or her supervisory function referred to in section 95 (1)(e).

(4) An appointment of a person as a special visitor or general visitor shall be made subject to such terms and conditions (including those relating to remuneration and allowances) as the Minister for Health, with the consent of the Minister for Public Expenditure and Reform, may determine.

(5) The Director may direct a special visitor or general visitor to visit—

(a) a decision-making assistant, co-decision-maker, decision-making representative, designated healthcare representative or attorney for a relevant person, or

(b) a relevant person for whom there is a decision-making assistant, co-decision-maker, decision-making representative, designated healthcare representative or attorney, or in respect of whom an order has been made under section 48,

and, subsequent to the visit, to submit to the Director a report on such matters concerning the person visited as the Director may specify in the direction.

(6) Subject to subsections (7) and (8), for the purposes of enabling the Director to perform his or her functions, he or she may direct a special visitor or general visitor to—

(a) at any reasonable time, examine and take copies of any health, personal welfare or financial record held in relation to a relevant person by any person, body or organisation, and

(b) interview a relevant person in private or otherwise than in public.

(7) Subsection (6) shall not entitle the Director to direct a general visitor to examine and take copies of any health record of a relevant person unless the general visitor is a registered medical practitioner.

(8) Prior to taking an action pursuant to paragraph (a) of subsection (6), the special visitor or general visitor, as the case may be, shall seek the consent of the relevant person to the taking of such action, unless the Director dispenses with this requirement where—

(a) there has been a declaration under section 37 (1)(b) in respect of the person, or

(b) an enduring power of attorney has been registered in respect of the person.

(9) A special visitor or general visitor shall not—

(a) attempt to obtain information that is not reasonably required for the purposes referred to in subsection (6), or

(b) use such information for a purpose that is not in accordance with this section.

(10) A special visitor or general visitor shall take reasonable steps to ensure that any information obtained pursuant to this section is—

(a) kept secure from unauthorised access, use or disclosure, and

(b) safely disposed of when he or she believes it is no longer required.

(11) The Director shall, on an annual basis, carry out checks to ascertain if special visitors and general visitors are complying with subsections (9) and (10).

ASSISTED DECISION-MAKING (CAPACITY) ACT 2015

PART 7

Interpretation

58. (1) In this Part—
"disqualified", in relation to an attorney, means the attorney becomes a person referred to in section 66 or a person that the court determines under this Part shall no longer act as attorney for the donor concerned;
"donor" has the meaning given to it in section 59 (1);
"donor under the Act of 1996" means a person who has created an enduring power under the Act of 1996;
"prescribed" means prescribed by regulations made by the Minister under section 79;
"trust corporation" has the meaning it has in section 30 of the Succession Act 1965 but shall not include a designated centre or mental health facility in which the donor resides.

(2) In this Part "person", in relation to an attorney, includes a trust corporation but only to the extent that the authority conferred under the enduring power of attorney relates to property and affairs.

General Note

Section 58 is a definition section. Note that "enduring power" is not defined here, but is defined in s.59(2).

Designated centre is defined in s.2 of the Act.

Subsection (2) provides for the definition of "person", in relation to an attorney, and reflects s.5(4)(a)(ii) in providing that a "person" includes a trust corporation, but only to the extent that the authority conferred under the enduring power relates to property and affairs. In the 1996 Act, this proviso does not apply.

The definition of "trust corporation" mirrors that in the 1996 Act, being a trust corporation within the meaning provided for in s.30 of the Succession Act 1965, with the proviso that it does not include a designated centre or mental health facility in which the donor of the power resides. Section 30 of the Succession Act 1965 provides in subs.(4) thereof as follows:

"In this Act, 'trust corporation' means—
- (a) a corporation appointed by the High Court in any particular case to be a trustee;
- (b) a corporation empowered by its constitution to undertake trust business, and having a place of business in the State or Northern Ireland, and being—
  - (i) a company established by Act or charter, or
  - (ii) an Associated Bank under the Central Bank Act 1942, or
  - (iii) a company (whether registered with or without limited liability) within the definition contained in the Companies Act 1963 or within the meaning of the corresponding law in Northern Ireland, having a capital (in stock or shares) for the time being issued of not less than £250,000, of which not less than £100,000 has been paid up in case, or
  - (iv) a company (registered without limited liability) within the definition contained in the said Companies Act or within the meaning of the said law of Northern Ireland, one of the members of which is a corporation within any of the previous provisions of this paragraph; or
- (c) a corporation which satisfies the President of the High Court that it undertakes the administration of any charitable, ecclesiastical or public trust without remuneration, or that by its constitution it is required to apply the whole of its net income for charitable, ecclesiastical or public purposes and is prohibited

from distributing, directly or indirectly, any part thereof by way of profits, and is authorised by the President of the High Court to act in relation to such trusts as a trust corporation."

The references to companies formed and registered under the Companies Act 1963 are to be read as references to companies formed and registered under that Act and under the Companies Act 2014, by virtue of s.6(1) of the Companies Act 2014.

Enduring power of attorney — general

59. (1) Subject to the provisions of this section and sections 60, 62 and 63, a person who has attained the age of 18 years (in this Act referred to as "donor") may appoint another person who has also attained that age (in this Act referred to as "attorney") on whom he or she confers either or both of the following:

(a) general authority to act on the donor's behalf in relation to all or a specified part of the donor's property and affairs; or

(b) authority to do specified things on the donor's behalf in relation to the donor's personal welfare or property and affairs, or both;

which may, in either case, be conferred subject to conditions and restrictions.

(2) The authority referred to in subsection (1) shall be known as an enduring power of attorney and shall be conferred in writing in an instrument which is in compliance with this Part and regulations made under section 79.

(3) A donor may, in an enduring power of attorney, appoint a person who shall act as attorney for the donor in respect of the relevant decisions specified therein in the event that an attorney on whom authority is conferred dies or is unable to act or is disqualified from acting as attorney.

(4) An enduring power of attorney shall not enter into force until—

(a) the donor lacks capacity in relation to one or more of the relevant decisions which are the subject of the power, and

(b) the instrument creating the enduring power of attorney has been registered in accordance with section 69.

(5) Where an enduring power of attorney is expressed to confer general authority in respect of all or a specified part of the donor's property and affairs, it operates to confer, subject to any restrictions provided in the power or in this Part, authority to do on behalf of the donor anything which the donor can lawfully do by attorney.

(6) A person is suitable for appointment as an attorney if he or she is able to perform the functions of attorney as specified in the enduring power of attorney.

General Note

Section 59 reflects some of the provisions of s.6 of the 1996 Act which deals with the scope and authority of an attorney under an enduring power of attorney. It specifies that a person (donor) can appoint another person (attorney) the general authority to act on his or her behalf in relation to a specified part of his or her property and affairs or an authority to do specified things on behalf of the donor in relation to the donor's personal welfare or property and affairs, or both. Unlike s.6, it does not contain a reference to "personal care decisions", but instead provides that the donor may confer authority "to do specified things on the donor's behalf in relation to the donor's welfare". "Personal welfare" and "property and affairs" are not defined in this section, but are set out in s.2 of the Act. The definition of "personal welfare" includes decisions on healthcare, which was not provided for under the 1996 Act.

Subsection 4 outlines that the enduring power of attorney shall not enter into force until the donor lacks capacity in relation to one or more decisions which are the subject of the power and the instrument creating the enduring power of attorney has been registered. The definition of capacity is set out in s.3 of the Act. The original Bill referred to "mental capacity", which has been amended to refer to "decision-making capacity" as set out in s.2 of the Act.

Before this Act came into force, "capacity" was not defined in legislation. Pursuant to s.3 of the 2015 Act, capacity must now be construed functionally. It sees a move away from a status based approach to a functional approach. The test for capacity is now to be assessed on an issued specific and time specific basis.

According to the Law Reform Commission, *Report on Vulnerable Adults and the Law* (LRC 83–2006):

> "The 'status' approach to capacity involves making a decision on a person's general legal capacity based on the presence or absence of certain characteristics. It usually involves an across-the-board assessment of a person's capacity based on disability, rather than the person's capacity in relation to the particular decision being made at a particular time. Under this approach, for example, a person who is in a long-stay psychiatric ward may be automatically denied capacity to make a will or to vote without regard to their actual capabilities. The status approach to capacity is evident in the Wards of Court system and in respect of enduring powers of attorney under the Powers of Attorney Act 1996, both of which involve a broad assessment of general legal capacity.
>
> A status approach to capacity has particular potential to operate inequitably in relation to persons whose capacity fluctuates. The status approach is also not appropriate for a person who, in the words of the Powers of Attorney Act 1996, 'is becoming mentally incapable' because clearly they have some cognitive ability and are capable of making some decisions. Neither is the status approach appropriate for a number of persons with intellectual disability who clearly have the capacity to make *some* decisions. The status approach was rejected by the Law Commission of England and Wales as being 'out of tune with the policy aim of enabling and encouraging people to take for themselves any decision which they have capacity to take'."

The LRC Report further outlined the definition of a function approach to capacity. "The 'functional' approach assesses capacity on an 'issue-specific' basis. Indeed, the question of legal capacity generally arises in a specific context—such as capacity to make a will, capacity to make a gift, to marry or to consent to medical treatment. In such circumstances the assessment of capacity is 'issue-specific'—therefore, a decision on legal capacity in relation to one issue will not necessarily be decided in the same manner in relation to another issue. The Commission notes that a 'functional' model of capacity is now the most widely accepted. An issue-specific, 'functional' approach to capacity assesses a person's capacity to make a particular decision. As a result, this model is in direct contrast to the all-or-nothing approach to capacity which tends to prevail under the status approach. In addition, the individual assessment of capacity which characterises the functional approach has the resulting benefit of involving a proportionate, minimum incursion on an individual's decision-making autonomy."

The LRC recommended that a predominantly functional approach should be taken in relation to legal capacity and this is now reflected in the Act.

Subsection (6) provides that a person is suitable for appointment to be an attorney if he or she is "able to perform the functions as specified in the enduring power of attorney". This provision does not exist in the 1996 Act although s.10(3)(d) thereof does provide that a notice of objection to the registration of an enduring power of attorney under the 1996 Act is valid if it is made on the ground that "... [h]aving regard to all the circumstances, the attorney is unsuitable to be the donor's attorney". Section 77 sets out what the Director should look at in determining if an attorney is "suitable" within the meaning of this section and includes the relationship and degree of connection between the donor and attorney, the degree of involvement which will be required on the part of the attorney in the care of the donor, the willingness of the attorney to carry out his or her functions and any conflict of interest that may arise. It seems possible that the provisions in the 2015 Act requiring the attorney to be "able to perform the functions of attorney as specified in the enduring power of attorney" could be construed as being more restrictive than the provision in s.10(3)(d) of the 1996 Act.

Content of instrument creating an enduring power of attorney

60. (1) An instrument creating an enduring power of attorney shall include the following statements:

(a) by the donor that he or she—

(i) understands the implications of creating the power,

(ii) intends the power to be effective at any subsequent time when he or she lacks capacity in relation to one or more relevant decisions which are the subject of the power, and

(iii) is aware that he or she may vary or revoke the power prior to its registration;

(b) by a legal practitioner that, after interviewing the donor and making any necessary enquiries, he or she—

(i) is satisfied that the donor understands the implications of creating the power,

(ii) is satisfied that the donor is aware that he or she may vary or revoke the power prior to its registration, and

(iii) has no reason to believe that the instrument is being executed by the donor as a result of fraud, coercion or undue pressure;

(c) by a registered medical practitioner that in his or her opinion at the time the power was executed, the donor had the capacity to understand the implications of creating the power;

(d) by a healthcare professional of a class that shall be prescribed, that in his or her opinion at the time the power was executed, the donor had the capacity to understand the implications of creating the power; and

(e) by the attorney, that he or she—

(i) understands the implications of undertaking to be an attorney for the donor and has read and understands the information contained in the instrument,

(ii) understands and undertakes to act in accordance with his or her functions as specified in the instrument creating the enduring power of attorney,

(iii) understands and undertakes to act in accordance with the guiding principles,

(iv) understands and undertakes to comply with the reporting obligations under section 75, and

(v) understands the requirements in relation to registration of the power.

(2) An instrument creating an enduring power of attorney shall include the following:

(a) the name, date of birth and contact details of the donor;

(b) subject to subsection (3), the signature of the donor and the date that he or she signed the power;

(c) the name, date of birth and contact details of the attorney;

(d) the signature of the attorney and the date that he or she signed the enduring power of attorney;

(e) the signatures of the 2 witnesses referred to in subsection (4)(a).

(3) An instrument creating an enduring power of attorney may be signed on behalf of the donor by a person who has attained the age of 18 years and who is not the attorney or a witness referred to in subsection (4)(a) if—

(a) the donor is unable to sign the instrument,

(b) the donor is present and directs that the instrument be signed on his or her behalf by that person, and

(c) the signature of the person is witnessed in accordance with subsection (4)(b).

(4)(a) The donor, or the person signing on his or her behalf in accordance with subsection (3), and the attorney shall sign the instrument creating the enduring power of attorney in the presence of each other and in the presence of 2 witnesses—

(i) each of whom has attained the age of 18 years,

(ii) of whom at least one is not an immediate family member of the donor or the attorney, and

(iii) neither of whom is an employee or agent of the attorney.

(b) Each of the witnesses referred to in paragraph (a) shall witness the signature of the donor (or the person signing on his or her behalf) and the signature of the attorney by applying his or her own signature to the instrument creating the enduring power of attorney.

(5) Where a donor proposes to remunerate an attorney for performing his or her functions as attorney, the instrument creating the enduring power of attorney shall specify the proposed remuneration and the functions to which it relates.

(6) In this section, "immediate family member" means—

(a) a spouse, civil partner, or cohabitant,

(b) a child, son-in-law or daughter-in-law,

(c) a parent, step-parent, mother-in-law or father-in-law,

(d) a brother, sister, step-brother, step-sister, brother-in-law or sister-in-law,

(e) a grandparent or grandchild,

(f) an aunt or uncle, or

(g) a nephew or niece.

General Note

Section 60 expands on some of the provisions of s.5 of the 1996 Act. The provisions set out in the Bill were broadly similar to the provisions under s.5. This section sets out what has to be included in an instrument which creates an enduring power of attorney. Subsection (1) states that the instrument must contain statements from the donor, a legal practitioner, a registered medical practitioner, a health care professional and the attorney in relation to various matters such as the capacity of the donor, that fraud, coercion or undue pressure was not used to create the enduring power and that the attorney is willing to undertake the functions of attorney under the power. Instead of only providing that the instrument creating the Enduring Power of Attorney must include a statement by the donor that he or she has read the information (or that it has been read to him or her) as to the effect of creating the power (which information was prescribed in S.I. No. 196 of 1996), s.60(1)(a) specifies in greater detail what must be in the donor's statement. Section 60(1)(b) also enlarges on the contents of the statement of the solicitor (now "legal practitioner") for the donor which now includes obligations on the legal practitioner to be "satisfied" that the donor understands the implications of creating the power and that the donor is aware that he or she may vary or revoke the power prior to its registration. The legal practitioner also has to state that he or she has no reason to believe that the power was executed as a result of fraud, coercion or undue pressure. There was no reference to "coercion" under the 1996 Act or the Bill. The statement of the registered medical practitioner, as referred to in subs.(1)(c), that the donor had the capacity to understand the implications (rather than "the effect", as provided in the 1996 Act) of creating the power, does not contain the qualification that the donor had the mental capacity "with the assistance of such explanations as may have been given to the donor, to understand the effect of creating the power".

It is obligatory to have such statements included in an instrument. There was no requirement in the Bill as originally drafted for statements from a "healthcare professional". Healthcare professional is defined in s.2 of the Act. The Minister for State at the Department of Health (Deputy Kathleen Lynch) stated:

> "It provides for an additional safeguard by requiring statements by two different professionals as to the capacity of the donor to understand the implications of creating such an enduring power. One of the statements must be from a health care professional such as a social worker so as to not be too reliant on the medical assessment of capacity." (244(6) *Seanad Éireann Debates* 9 December 2015).

The provisions of subs.(1)(e) regarding the statement by the attorney in the enduring power are wider than those in the corresponding provision of the 1996 Act (s.5(2)(d)(iv)) and includes specific undertakings by the attorney which were not provided for in the 1996 Act. This broadening of the statement to be made by the attorney was one of the very few amendments made to this part of the Bill at Committee Stage of the *Dáil*. In relation to s.60(1)(e), the Minister for State for the Department of Health (Deputy Kathleen Lynch) stated: "This provision is intended as an extra safeguard to ensure that the attorney makes a commitment in advance of being appointed as attorney, to act in accordance with the functions of the attorney, which include the obligations arising under this Bill. This is to ensure that there is no ambiguity as to the attorney's agreement and willingness to abide by the obligations arising for the attorney under this Bill" (Select Committee on Justice, Defence and Equality Debate, Vol.2, No.45). The Attorney must undertake to act in accordance with the guiding principles. An attorney is listed as an "intervener" in s.2(1)(b) of the 2015 Act. The guiding principles are set out in s.8 of the Act. The guiding principles, which do not apply to instruments under the 1996 Act, provide further safeguards and protections to donors under the 2015 Act. The Minister for State at the Department of Health (Deputy Kathleen Lynch) stated, "The guiding principles apply to every intervention. They are intended to embed the ethos that the person's autonomy is to be safeguarded to the greatest extent possible" (Second Stage *Dáil Éireann* Debate). They place the common law presumption of capacity on a statutory basis and provide that a donor should be involved, in so far as is practicable, in the decision-making process.

Section 60 also specifies, in subs.(2), certain further contents to be included in the enduring power (some of which were specified in S.I. No. 196 of 1996 rather than in the 1996 Act). It was envisaged in the Bill that these would be left to Regulations. Subsection (3) sets out the circumstances where an instrument creating an enduring power of attorney may be signed by someone other than the donor. According to The Minister for State at the Department of Health (Deputy Kathleen Lynch): "The NDA advised that the Bill needed to provide for situations where, due to literacy issues, blindness, dexterity, etc., a person was unable to sign a document. The proposed provisions that will apply where a person cannot sign the document accords with advice that such a situation will require the combined input of the donor, the attorney, the substitute signatory and two witnesses" (244(6) *Seanad Éireann Debates* 9 December 2015). Subsection (4) relates to the provisions regarding the witnessing of an instrument creating an enduring power. It states that donor and the attorney shall sign the instrument in the presence of each other. This is likely to cause practical difficulties. This was not a requirement under the 1996 Act. There is in this subsection specific provision as to the status of the witnesses which was not contained in the 1996 Act, including a provision that a witness cannot be an "immediate family member". The Minister for State at the Department of Health (Deputy Kathleen Lynch) states: "The requirement that at least one witness not be an immediate family member is to provide an additional safeguard in order that an independent person must be involved as a witness. This is to reduce the risk of a donor being pushed by family members into conferring an enduring power of attorney against his or her wishes." (244(6) *Seanad Éireann Debates* 9 December 2015). Subsection (6) defines "immediate family member", which includes a cohabitant, and "a child, son-in-law or daughter-in-law", but interestingly, does not include the son or daughter of a cohabitant. It is certainly arguable that the enhanced provisions of s.60 unnecessarily complicate and overburden the making of an enduring power.

Notice of execution of an enduring power of attorney

61. (1) The donor shall, as soon as practicable after the execution of the instrument creating the enduring power of attorney, give notice, in such form as shall be prescribed, of such execution to the following persons:

(a) a spouse or civil partner of the donor;
(b) the cohabitant (if any) of the donor;
(c) any children of the donor who have attained the age of 18 years;
(d) any decision-making assistant for the donor;
(e) any co-decision-maker for the donor;
(f) any decision-making representative for the donor;
(g) any designated healthcare representative for the donor;
(h) any other attorney for the donor or attorney under the Act of 1996 in respect of the donor;
(i) any other person or persons as may be specified by the donor in the instrument creating the enduring power of attorney as a person or persons to whom notice shall be given under this section and section 68 (3).

(2) Where there are fewer than 3 persons to whom notice may be given pursuant to subsection (1), the donor shall specify 2 persons in the instrument creating the enduring power of attorney as persons to whom notice shall be given under this section and section 68 (3).

General Note

Section 61 sets out the notification requirements in relation to the execution of an enduring power of attorney. A similar provision was contained in the First Schedule to the 1996 Act (see p.48), rather than in the body of that Act. However, the provisions of s.61 are more extensive. This section requires the donor to give, as soon as practicable after the execution of the instrument, notice of the execution of the power to all close family members such as a spouse and children over 18 years of age, and any decision-making supporters that the donor may have such as a decision-making assistant or co-decision-maker. It also provides that the donor shall name two other persons whom he or she wishes to inform of the execution of the enduring power where there are fewer than three people to who notice may be given pursuant to subs.(1). Under the provisions of the 1996 Act, it was only necessary for one of the notice parties to be a spouse, child or relative as defined in the First Schedule thereto. Oddly, this section does not prescribe other relatives as notice parties where there are none of the foregoing.

Scope of authority — personal welfare decisions

62. (1) Where an enduring power of attorney confers authority in relation to personal welfare, the power does not authorise an attorney to do an act that is intended to restrain the donor unless there are exceptional emergency circumstances and—

(a) the donor lacks capacity in relation to the matter in question or the attorney reasonably believes that the donor lacks such capacity,

(b) the attorney reasonably believes that it is necessary to do the act in order to prevent an imminent risk of serious harm to the donor or to another person, and

(c) the act is a proportionate response to the likelihood of the harm referred to in paragraph (b) and to the seriousness of such harm.

(2) For the purposes of this section, an attorney restrains a donor if he or she—

(a) uses, or indicates an intention to use, force to secure the doing of an act which the donor resists,

(b) intentionally restricts the donor's liberty of voluntary movement or behaviour, whether or not the donor resists,

(c) administers a medication, which is not necessary for a medically identified condition, with the intention of controlling or modifying the donor's behaviour or ensuring that he or she is compliant or not capable of resistance, or

(d) authorises another person to do any of the things referred to in paragraph (a) to (c).

(3) An attorney who restrains a donor shall cease the restraint immediately upon the restraint no longer being necessary in order to prevent an imminent risk of serious harm to the donor or to another person.

(4) Subsections (1) to (3) shall not be construed to prejudice the generality of section 69 of the Mental Health Act 2001 or of rules made under that section.

(5) A donor shall not, in an enduring power of attorney, include a relevant decision—

(a) relating to refusal of life-sustaining treatment, or

(b) which is the subject of an advanced healthcare directive made by him or her.

(6) To the extent that an enduring power of attorney includes a relevant decision specified in subsection (5), the power shall be null and void.

General Note

Section 62 regulates personal welfare decisions in relation to the restraining of donors of enduring powers. The Minister for State at the Department of Health (Deputy Kathleen Lynch) stated: "As with all other interveners, restraint by attorneys is to be tightly regulated and only used in limited circumstances. The situation has to be an exceptional emergency in which there is an imminent risk of serious harm to the donor or to another person" (244(6) *Seanad Éireann Debates* 9 December 2015). The donor must lack capacity at the time of the restraint in relation to the matter in question or the attorney must reasonably believe that the donor lacks capacity and the act must be a proportionate response to the likelihood of harm. Subsection (2) defines "restrains" as an action that is intentional and designed to restrict voluntary movements rather than involuntary ones, such as spasm. It includes the definition of chemical restraint in that definition. This was not provided for in the Bill and was inserted at Report Stage in the *Dáil*. Subsection (3) provides that the restraint be immediately stopped when no longer necessary. Subsection (4) provides that subss.(1) to (3) shall not constrain the generality of s.69 of the Mental Health Act 2001 or of Rules made under that section, which states:

> "(1) A person shall not place a patient in seclusion or apply mechanical means of bodily restraint to the patient unless such seclusion or restraint is determined, in accordance with the rules made under *subsection (2)*, to be necessary for the purposes of treatment or to prevent the patient from injuring himself or herself or others and unless the seclusion or restraint complies with such rules.

(2) The Commission shall make rules providing for the use of seclusion and mechanical means of bodily restraint on a patient.

(3) A person who contravenes this section or a rule made under this section shall be guilty of an offence and shall be liable on summary conviction to a fine not exceeding £1,500.

(4) In this section "patient" includes—

(a) a child in respect of whom an order under section 25 is in force, and

(b) a voluntary patient."

Subsection (5) prevents a donor from authorising an attorney from making a decision relating to the refusal of life-sustaining treatment or from making a decision that is the subject of an advance health care directive by the donor. Although healthcare decisions can be made by attorneys, the High Court has jurisdiction in relation to applications for the withdrawal of life sustaining treatment pursuant to s.4(3)(b) of the Act. Subsection (6) states that if an enduring power contains a relevant decision relating to the refusal of life-sustaining treatment or a decision that is the subject of an advance health care directive, the power is null and void to the extent that it relates to that decision.

Scope of authority — property and affairs

63. (1) An attorney may act under an enduring power of attorney relating to property and affairs for the attorney's benefit or that of other persons to the extent provided for in the power, where specific provision to that effect is made in the power and subject to any conditions or restrictions contained in the power.

(2) An attorney may not dispose of the property of the donor by way of gift unless specific provision to that effect is made in the enduring power of attorney.

(3) Where an enduring power of attorney authorises the disposal of the donor's property by way of gift, the attorney's power to make such gifts shall, in addition to being subject to any conditions or restrictions in the enduring power, be limited to—

(a) gifts made on customary occasions to persons (including the attorney) who are related to or connected to the donor and in relation to whom the donor might be expected to make gifts, and

(b) gifts to any charity to which the donor made or might be expected to make gifts,

provided that the value of the gift is reasonable having regard to all the circumstances and in particular the extent of the donor's assets and any financial obligations.

General Note

Section 63 refers to the scope of the attorney's authority in relation to the donor's "property and affairs" and is similar to the corresponding provisions in s.6 of the 1996 Act. Its provision regarding disposals of property by the attorney by way of gift differs from the corresponding provision in s.6(5)(a) of the 1996 Act in providing that the gifts shall be limited to gifts made on "customary occasions", rather than those "of a seasonal nature or at a time, or (made) on an anniversary, of a birth or marriage". This section was amended at Committee Stage of the Dail to "prevent attorneys from considering themselves permitted to engage in extensive gift giving from the donor's assets and income" (Select Committee on Justice, Defence and Equality Debate, Vol.2 No.45). It provides that the attorney may, if specific provision to that effect is made in the power, act for his or her own benefit or that of any other person's benefit to the extent provided for in the power. Subsections (2) and (3) refer to the giving of gifts by the attorney on behalf of the donor. The donor must specify in the power that the attorney may give gifts, while subs.(3) limits these gifts to customary occasions and to persons, including the attorney, to whom the donor would have likely given gifts in the past. Customary occasions are defined in s.2 of the Act. The value of the gifts must be reasonable, taking the circumstances of the donor into consideration. Subsection 3(b) was amended at Committee Stage of the *Dáil* to include the reference to the donor's financial obligation. This is not included in the 1996 Act. The Minister for State at the Department of Health (Deputy Kathleen Lynch) indicated that this is to ensure, "that account be taken to the financial obligations of the person lacking capacity, as well as assets, when deciding whether it is appropriate to give gifts. If a person were to have extensive financial obligations, for instance, it would be important that such obligations would be honoured first before engaging in gift giving" (Select Committee on Justice, Defence and Equality Debate Vol.2 No.45).

Application to joint and joint and several attorneys

64. (1) A donor may, in an enduring power of attorney, appoint more than one attorney and may specify that the attorneys shall act—

(a) jointly,

(b) jointly and severally, or

(c) jointly in respect of some matters and jointly and severally in respect of other matters,

and, in default of the power so specifying, the attorneys shall be deemed to have authority to act jointly.

(2) Where 2 or more persons have authority to act jointly as attorneys, then, in the case of the death, lack of capacity or disqualification of any one or more of them, the remaining attorney or attorneys may continue to act, whether solely or jointly, as the case may be, unless the enduring power expressly provides to the contrary.

General Note

Section 64 details provisions regarding attorneys being appointed to act jointly, jointly and severally, or jointly in respect of some matters and severally in respect of others. In default of the power so specifying, the attorneys shall be presumed to have authority to act jointly. These provisions were not contained in the 1996 Act.

Persons who are not eligible to be attorneys

65. (1) A person shall not be eligible for appointment as an attorney under an enduring power of attorney if he or she—

(a) has been convicted of an offence in relation to the person or property of the person who intends to appoint an attorney,

(b) has been the subject of a safety or barring order in relation to the person who intends to appoint an attorney,

(c) is an undischarged bankrupt or is currently in a debt settlement arrangement or personal insolvency arrangement or has been convicted of an offence involving fraud or dishonesty,

(d) is a person in respect of whom a declaration under section 819 of the Act of 2014 has been made or is deemed to be subject to such a declaration by virtue of Chapter 5 of Part 14 of that Act,

(e) is a person who is subject or is deemed to be subject to a disqualification order, within the meaning of Chapter 4 of Part 14 of the Act of 2014, by virtue of that Chapter or any other provisions of that Act,

(f) is a person who is—

(i) the owner or the registered provider of a designated centre or

mental health facility in which the intending donor resides, or
(ii) residing with, or an employee or agent of, such owner or registered provider,

unless the person is a spouse, civil partner, cohabitant, parent, child or sibling of the intending donor, or

(g) has been convicted of an offence under section 34, 80, 90 or 145.

(2) Subsection (1)(c), (d) and (e) shall not apply where it is proposed to confer authority only in relation to personal welfare matters.

General Note

Section 65 is an updated and expanded version of the corresponding provision in the 1996 Act (s.5(4)) relating to persons who are not eligible to be attorneys in enduring powers). One of the additions to the categories of persons who are not eligible for appointment as attorneys is a person who "has been the subject of a safety or barring order in relation to the person who intends to appoint an attorney". Section 7 of the 1996 Act had provided that, unless the power otherwise provided, an enduring power shall be invalidated or cease to be in force, as the case may be, "a protection order, interim barring order, barring order or safety order is made against the attorney on the application of the donor, or vice versa".

The Act does not deal with the question of the ineligibility of trust corporations, which are included in the definition of "person" in s.58(2). However, a trust corporation controlled by a natural person who is not eligible for appointment to be an attorney could hardly be considered "suitable" for appointment as such—see s.71(2)(f).

Disqualification of attorney

66. (1) An attorney shall, with effect from the date on which an event specified in any of paragraphs (a) to (c) occurs or, in the case of an event specified in paragraph (d), at the expiry of the period referred to in that paragraph, and unless the instrument creating the enduring power of attorney provides otherwise, be disqualified from being an attorney for the donor where the attorney is the spouse of the donor and subsequently—

(a) the marriage is annulled or dissolved either—
(i) under the law of the State, or
(ii) under the law of another state and is, by reason of that annulment or dissolution, not or no longer a subsisting valid marriage under the law of the State,

(b) a decree of judicial separation is granted to either spouse by a court in the State or any decree is so granted by a court outside the State and is recognised in the State as having like effect,

(c) a written agreement to separate is entered into between the spouses, or

(d) subject to section 2(2), the spouses separate and cease to cohabit for a continuous period of 12 months.

(2) An attorney shall, with effect from the date on which an event specified in paragraph (a) or (b) occurs or, in the case of an event specified in paragraph (c), at the expiry of the period referred to in that paragraph, and unless the instrument creating the enduring power of attorney provides otherwise, be disqualified from being attorney for the donor where the attorney is the civil partner of the donor and subsequently—

(a) the civil partnership is annulled or dissolved (other than where the dissolution occurs by virtue of the parties to that civil partnership marrying each other) either—

(i) under the law of the State, or

(ii) under the law of another state and is, by means of that annulment or dissolution not or no longer a subsisting valid civil partnership under the law of the State,

(b) a written agreement to separate is entered into between the civil partners, or

(c) subject to section 2(2), the civil partners separate and cease to cohabit for a continuous period of 12 months.

(3) Subject to section 2(2), an attorney shall, at the expiry of the period referred to in this subsection, and unless the instrument creating the enduring power of attorney provides otherwise, be disqualified from being an attorney for the donor where the attorney is the cohabitant of the donor and subsequently the cohabitants separate and cease to cohabit for a continuous period of 12 months.

(4) Subject to subsection (5), where, subsequent to the appointment of an attorney—

(a) the attorney is convicted of an offence in relation to the person or property of the donor or the person or property of a child of the donor,

(b) a safety or barring order is made against the attorney in relation to the donor or a child of the donor,

(c) the attorney becomes an undischarged bankrupt or subject to a debt settlement arrangement or personal insolvency arrangement which is current or is convicted of an offence involving fraud or dishonesty,

(d) the attorney becomes a person in respect of whom a declaration has been made under section 819 of the Act of 2014 or is deemed to be subject to such a declaration by virtue of Chapter 5 of Part 14 of that Act,

(e) the attorney becomes a person who is subject or is deemed to be subject to a disqualification order within the meaning of Chapter 4 of Part 14 of the Act of 2014 by virtue of that Chapter or any other provisions of that Act,

(f) the attorney becomes—

(i) the owner or the registered provider of a designated centre or mental health facility in which the intending donor resides, or

(ii) a person residing with, or an employee or agent of, a person referred to in sub paragraph (i),

unless the person is a spouse, civil partner, cohabitant, parent, child or sibling of the intending donor,

(g) the attorney is convicted of an offence under section 34, 80, 90 or 145,

(h) the attorney—

(i) enters into a decision-making assistance agreement as a relevant person,

(ii) enters into a co-decision-making agreement as a relevant person,

(iii) has an enduring power of attorney or an enduring power under the Act of 1996 registered in respect of himself or herself, or

(iv) becomes the subject of a declaration under section 37 (1), or

(i) the attorney is a trust corporation and the trust corporation is dissolved, the attorney shall be disqualified from being an attorney for the donor with effect from the day on which the attorney falls within any of paragraphs (a) to (i).

(5) Subsections (4)(c), (d) and (e) shall not apply to an attorney insofar as authority is conferred on him or her under the enduring power of attorney in relation to personal welfare matters.

(6) Where an attorney becomes disqualified under this section, he or she, or in the case of disqualification pursuant to subsection (4)(h)(iii) or (iv), his or her attorney, decision-making representative or the court, as the case may be, shall notify the Director of such disqualification and the particulars relating thereto.

(7) Where an attorney becomes disqualified, a relevant decision made solely by him or her after his or her disqualification shall be null and void.

(8) Subsection (7) shall not operate to prevent a person who relied on a relevant decision referred to in that subsection from recovering damages in respect of any loss incurred by him or her as a result of that reliance.

General Note

Section 66 replaces the provisions of s.5(6) and (7) of the 1996 Act (see p.12) regarding the invalidity of enduring powers in certain circumstances such as the bankruptcy of the attorney or the annulment of the marriage of the donor and the attorney. Section 66 takes a different approach and provides for the disqualification of the attorney (but not the invalidity of the enduring power) on the occurrence of certain events.

Subsection (1)(a) provides that the attorney shall be disqualified from being an attorney for the donor, unless the power provides otherwise, where the attorney is the spouse of the donor and where subsequently their marriage is annulled or dissolved in the State, or under the law of another state and is no longer a valid and subsisting marriage under the law of the State.

Subsection (1)(b) provides for a similar disqualification where a decree of judicial separation is granted in the State, or by a court outside the State and is recognised in the State as having like effect.

Subsection (1)(c) provides for a similar disqualification where the spouses have entered into a separation agreement, and subs.(1)(d) disqualifies the attorney where the spouses separate and cease to cohabit for a continuous period of 12 months.

Subsection (2) makes similar provisions for civil partners.

Subsection (3) makes a similar provision for when cohabitants (as defined in s.2) separate and cease to cohabit for a continuous period of 12 months

There is no similar provision to cover people cohabiting (for example people of the same sex) who are not cohabitants as defined in s.2.

Subsection (4) provides for further circumstances for the disqualification of an attorney, which cannot be overridden by a provision to the contrary in the power. Subsection 4(a) provides for disqualification where the attorney has been convicted of an offense in relation to the person or property of the donor of a child of the donor (but makes no such provision where the offense relates to other relations of the donor such as brothers or sisters). Subsection 4(b) provides for disqualification where a safety or barring order is made against the attorney in relation to the donor or a child of the donor (but again there is no reference to any other relation, nor is there any provision for a situation where an injunction is granted by a court in favour of the donor or in respect of a child or other relation of the donor against the attorney). Subsection 4(c) refers to disqualifications in circumstances of bankruptcy, fraud or dishonesty. Subsection 4(d) provides for disqualification where a declaration has been made under s.819 of the Companies Act 2014 or where an attorney is deemed to be subject to such a disqualification by virtue of Chapter 5 of Part 14 of that Act.

Subsection 4(e) disqualifies an attorney where the attorney becomes a person who is subject or is deemed to be subject to a disqualification order within the meaning of Ch.4 of Pt 14 of the Companies Act 2014. Section 838 of that Act provides as follows:

"Meaning of 'disqualified' and 'disqualification order'

838. In this Chapter—

'disqualification order' means an order of the court that a person shall be disqualified;

'disqualified', in relation to a person, means the person's being disqualified from being appointed or acting as a director or other officer, statutory auditor, receiver, liquidator or examiner or being in any way, whether directly or indirectly, concerned or taking part in the promotion, formation or management of each of the following:

(a) a company within the meaning of *section 819(6)*;

(b) any friendly society within the meaning of the Friendly Societies Acts 1896 to 2014;

(c) any society registered under the Industrial and Provident Societies Acts 1893 to 2014."

Subsection 4(f) provides that an attorney is disqualified where he or she becomes the owner or the registered provider of a designated centre or mental health facility in which the "intending" donor resides, or where the attorney becomes a person residing with, or an employee or agent of such owner or registered provider, unless the attorney of a spouse, civil partner, cohabitant, parent, child or sibling of the "intending" donor. It is interesting that "sibling" is included here but not in subs.4(a) and (b). Subsection 4(g) provides for the disqualification of attorneys who are convicted of an offense under ss.34, 80, 90 or 145 of the 2015 Act—see Appendix to Pt 2.

Subsection 4(h) provides for the disqualification of an attorney where the attorney enters into a decision-making assistance agreement as a relevant person (see s.10 in Appendix to Pt 2); enters into a co-decision-making agreement as a relevant person (see s.17 in Appendix to Pt 2); has an enduring power of attorney (under either the 1996 Act or the 2015 Act) registered in respect of himself or herself; becomes the subject of a declaration under s.37(1) (see section in Appendix to Pt 2); or where the attorney is a trust corporation which has been dissolved.

Subsection (5) provides that subs.4(c), (d) and (e) do not apply to an attorney insofar as authority is conferred on him or her in relation to personal welfare matters. It is therefore possible for an attorney to be disqualified from acting as attorney in respect of some decisions, but not in respect of other decisions. This distinction did not appear in the 1996 Act. The reference to a decision-making representative in subs.(6) is to a person appointed by the court pursuant to s.38(2) of the Act of 2015 "for the purposes of making one or more than one decision specified in the order on behalf of the relevant person in relation to his or her personal welfare or property and affairs or both". Subsection 7 provides that where an attorney becomes disqualified, a relevant decision made solely by him or her after such disqualification shall be null and void. Subsection (8) provides that subs.(7) shall not operate to prevent a person who relied on a relevant decision referred to in that subsection from recovering damages in respect of any loss incurred by him or her as a result of that reliance. See references to ss.13 and 18 of the 1996 Act, pp.26 and 31 in relation to the protection given by these sections.

The Act of 2015 does not deal with the question of the disqualification of trust corporations, which are included in the definition of "person" in s.58(2). However, a trust corporation controlled by a natural person who could be disqualified by the provisions of s.66 could hardly be considered "suitable" to continue to act as an attorney—see s.71(2)(f).

Function of court prior to registration

67. On application to it by any interested party, the court may, where it has reason to believe that the donor of an enduring power of attorney lacks capacity in relation to one or more relevant decisions, exercise any power which would become exercisable under section 77 (3) on the registration of the instrument creating an enduring power of attorney and may do so whether or not the attorney concerned has made an application to the Director for registration of the instrument.

General Note

Section 67 deals with the functions of the court prior to registration of an enduring power of attorney. This section reflects the provisions in s.8 of the 1996 Act. It permits the court to exercise any power which would become exercisable under s.77(3) on the registration of the enduring power. An application to the courts in relation to this can be made by any interested party whether or not the attorney has made an application for registration. The relevant court referred to in the original Bill was the High Court. This was amended at Committee Stage of the Seanad and the court referred to in this section, and all sections of this part, is the Circuit Court.

Application for registration of instrument creating enduring power

68. (1) Where an attorney has reason to believe that the donor lacks capacity in relation to one or more relevant decisions which are the subject of the enduring power of attorney, the attorney shall, as soon as is practicable, make an application, in compliance with this Part and regulations made under section 79, to the Director to register the instrument creating the enduring power of attorney.

(2) An application to register an instrument under subsection (1) shall be made in such form and accompanied by such fee as shall be prescribed.

(3) The attorney shall, at the same time as he or she makes an application under subsection (1), give notice, in such form as shall be prescribed, of the application and give a copy of the instrument creating an enduring power of attorney to the following persons:

(a) the donor;
(b) a spouse or civil partner (if any) of the donor;
(c) the cohabitant (if any) of the donor;
(d) any children of the donor who have attained the age of 18 years;
(e) any decision-making assistant for the donor;
(f) any co-decision-maker for the donor;
(g) any decision-making representative for the donor;
(h) any designated healthcare representative for the donor;
(i) any other attorney for the donor or attorney under the Act of 1996 in respect of the donor;
(j) any other person specified by the donor under section 61.

(4) An attorney may, before making an application to register an instrument creating an enduring power of attorney, apply to the court for a determination on any question as to the validity of the power.

(5) Where an attorney has made an application to register an instrument creating an enduring power of attorney, then pending determination of the application, the attorney, or if more than one attorney has been appointed to act jointly or jointly and severally, as the case may be, any one of them, may take action under the power—

(a) to maintain the donor or prevent loss to the donor's assets,
(b) to the extent permitted by the enduring power, to make a relevant decision which cannot reasonably be deferred until the application has been determined, or
(c) to maintain the attorney or other persons in so far as that is permitted under the power.

(6) Following the taking of an action pursuant to subsection (5), an attorney

shall report to the Director—

(a) what action he or she took,

(b) the reasons as to why the action could not be deferred until after the registration of the instrument creating the enduring power of attorney,

(c) any measures he or she took to encourage the donor to participate in the action taken, and

(d) the outcome of the action.

(7) An application to register an instrument creating an enduring power of attorney shall be accompanied by—

(a) the instrument creating the enduring power of attorney,

(b) a statement by a registered medical practitioner and a statement by such other healthcare professional of a class as shall be prescribed that in their opinion the donor lacks capacity in relation to one or more relevant decisions which are the subject of the enduring power,

(c) details of any existing decision-making assistance agreement, co-decision-making agreement, decision-making order, decision-making representation order, power of attorney (whether an enduring power or otherwise and whether registered or not) or advance healthcare directive in respect of the appointer,

(d) a copy of any notice given pursuant to subsection (3),

(e) a copy of any notice given pursuant to section 61, and

(f) the prescribed fee.

(8) Where there is more than one attorney appointed under an enduring power of attorney, any two or more of the attorneys may make a joint application to register the instrument.

General Note

Section 68 deals with applications for registration of the instrument creating an enduring power of attorney. The Minister for State at the Department of Health (Deputy Kathleen Lynch) stated that:

> "[A]dditional text has been added (to the original Bill) to incorporate provisions that were to be provided for by way of regulations and to strengthen the safeguards against the premature or fraudulent registration of an enduring power. It sets out the obligations placed on the attorney when he or she has reason to believe the donor lacks capacity in relation to one or more relevant decisions which are the subject of the enduring power" (244(6) *Seanad Éireann Debates* 9 December 2015).

This section corresponds with s.9 of the 1996 Act with notable differences. In subs.(1) of s.9, the duty on the attorney to apply for the registration of the enduring power was triggered by the attorney having reason to believe that the donor is or is becoming mentally incapable. However, subs.(1) of s.68 imposes that duty on the attorney where the attorney "has reason to believe that the donor lacks capacity in relation to one or more relevant decisions which are the subject of the enduring power of attorney". Powers of attorney under the 1996 Act which have not yet been registered will continue to be registered when the donor "is or is becoming mentally incapable", whereas registrations of instruments under this Act shall be when the donor "lacks capacity in relation to one or more decision".

The application for registration under s.9 was to the court (in practise to the Office of Wards of Court), whereas under s.68 it is to the Director of the Decision Support Service of the Mental Health Commission (the "Director") (see s.94 of the 2015 Act in the definitions section). The original Bill provided for the Director of the Decision Support Services, or the Office of the Public Guardian, as it was referred, to be based in the Court Services. There was considerable parliamentary debate in relation to this. The Government concluded it would be more appropriate to move the responsibility for the Decision Support Service from the

Court Service to the Mental Health Commission in December 2015. The Minister stated:

> "The original decision to locate the Office of Public Guardianship, as it was then called, in the Court Service was based on the view that the Office of Wards of Court could form the kernel of the staff of the new body. However, stakeholders have pointed to the desirability of moving away from the Office of Wards of Court to avoid the false impression that wardship could be perpetuated by another name" (244(9) *Seanad Éireann Debates* 15 December 2015).

The application for registration is to be in accordance with regulations under s.79. Subsection (3) provides for the giving of notice, and a copy of the enduring power, at the same time as the application for registration is made, in prescribed form, to those listed therein, several of whom are included in those classes of persons who were entitled to receive notice under s.9(3) of the 1996 Act and set out in the First Schedule thereto. However, it is noteworthy that the First Schedule to the 1996 Act prescribed that those entitled to receive notice included the donor's brothers and sisters, grandchildren, and children of the donor's brothers and sisters, and the widow or widower of a child of the donor. These are not included in s.68(3). Instead, there is a provision in subs.(3)(j) that notice can be given to "any other person specified by the donor under section 61". One might question the exclusion of these classes. While the First Schedule to the 1996 Act provided for the giving of notice usually to no more than three persons, s.68(3) provides for the giving of notice to all those specified therein, who are those to whom notice of the making of the enduring power has been given. Similar to the 1996 Act, the Bill referred to notice parties being listed in the Schedule. According to The Minister for State at the Department of Health (Deputy Kathleen Lynch):

> "The provisions and the accompanying regulations have been a source of confusion and conflict in recent years. In order to simplify and to provide protection against premature or fraudulent registration, I propose that all close family members be notified by the attorney that he or she intends to register the enduring power. Those notified will then have the opportunity to object to the registration if they are of the opinion that the attorney is not suitable or that undue pressure was placed on the donor to choose the appointed attorney. The amended notification provisions in this new section, coupled with the new notification requirements at execution stage, should, I hope, ensure all of those who need to be informed of an enduring power of attorney are notified" (244(6) *Seanad Éireann Debates* 9 December 2015).

Subsection (5) is in similar terms to s.7(2) of the 1996 Act in that it permits the attorney to take certain action under the enduring power where the attorney has applied for registration of the enduring power but the application for registration has not been determined. Under subs.(6) the attorney must, following taking any such action, make a report thereon in accordance with that subsection to the Director. This, or a similar, provision did not appear in the 1996 Act.

Subsection (7) provides for the documents to accompany the application for registration. These include statements made by a registered medical practitioner and a prescribed healthcare professional that in their opinion the donor lacks capacity in relation to one or more relevant decisions which are the subject of the enduring power. There is no provision as to what happens if these disagree, such as, for example, an application to the Director.

Subsection (8) provides that where there is more than one attorney, any two or more can make a joint application to register the instrument.

Registration of an instrument creating an enduring power of attorney

69. (1) On receipt of an application under section 68, the Director shall review the application and any objections received under section 71 and shall carry out such reasonable enquiries as he or she considers necessary in order to establish whether the following criteria are met:

(a) the enduring power of attorney and the instrument creating it are in accordance with sections 59, 60, 62 and 63;

(b) the attorney is a suitable person within the meaning of section 59 (6);

(c) the attorney is eligible for appointment within the meaning of section 65 or not disqualified by virtue of section 66;

(d) notice has been given in accordance with section 61 and section 68 (3); and

(e) the application is in accordance with section 68.

(2) Where, after reviewing an application under section 68, the Director is satisfied that the application is in order, he or she shall, subject to section 71, register the instrument creating the enduring power of attorney.

(3) Where, after reviewing an application under section 68, the Director forms the view that one or more of the criteria in paragraphs (a) to (e) of subsection (1) are not satisfied, he or she shall notify the attorney and the donor of his or her view, provide reasons for that view and give the attorney and the donor an opportunity, within a reasonable timeframe specified by the Director, to respond.

(4) Following a review of any response received pursuant to subsection (3), the Director shall—

(a) where he or she is of the view that the criteria set out in paragraphs (a) to (e) of subsection (1) are satisfied, register, subject to section 71, the instrument creating the enduring power of attorney, or

(b) where he or she remains of the view that one or more of the criteria set out in paragraphs (a) to (e) of subsection (1) is not satisfied, refuse to register the instrument creating the enduring power of attorney and notify the attorney and the donor of that fact and the reasons for his or her view.

(5) An attorney whose application under section 68 is refused may, not later than 21 days after the date of issue of the notification of refusal by the Director, appeal the refusal to the court.

(6) Upon an appeal under subsection (5), the court may—

(a) require the Director to register the instrument creating the enduring power of attorney,

(b) affirm the decision of the Director, or

(c) make such other order or declaration as it considers appropriate.

(7) Following registration of an instrument creating an enduring power of attorney, the Director shall send an authenticated copy of the instrument to the attorney and the donor.

(8) A document purporting to be a copy of an instrument creating an enduring power of attorney which has been authenticated by the Director shall be evidence of the contents of the instrument and the date upon which it was registered.

General Note

Section 69 deals with the registration of instruments creating enduring power of attorney. It lists the criteria that the director is obliged to consider when reviewing an application to register an enduring power. Subsection (2) provides that, subject to any objection received under s.71, where the director is satisfied that the application is in order, he or she shall register the instrument creating the power.

Subsection (3) provides that, where the director is of the view that one or more of the criteria in subs.(1) are not satisfied, he or she shall notify the attorney and the donor of his or her view and give the attorney and the donor the opportunity to respond. The Minister for State at the Department of Health (Deputy Kathleen Lynch) stated: "This is a new provision that allows the attorney or donor to provide further material or evidence to back up the application for registration because we cannot rule out the possibility of vexatious complaints about who is chosen" (244(6) *Seanad Éireann Debates* 9 December 2015).

Subsection (4) provides that following the receipt of further information or material as provided for in subs.(3), the director can either register the instrument if he or she is satisfied that the criteria listed in subs.(1) have been met or refuse to register the instrument because the criteria are not deemed to have been met.

Subsection (5) provides for an appeals mechanism for an attorney whose application to register is refused. It sets out a time-limit of 21 days from the time the attorney is notified that the application has been refused to appeal the decision of the director to the court.

Subsection (6) outlines what the court may do upon an appeal under subs.(5). The court may require the director to register the instrument, or affirm the director's decision to refuse to register it or make an order or declaration, as it considers appropriate. The court referred to in this section, and in all sections of this Act which apply to Enduring Powers of Attorneys, is the Circuit Court. The is provided for in s.4 of the Act, which outlines that the Circuit Court is to have exclusive jurisdiction under the Act except for certain matters referred to the High Court. Under the original Bill, the High Court had jurisdiction in relation to Enduring Powers of Attorney. For enduring powers created under the 1996 Act, the High Court retains jurisdiction. However, if a complaint is made about an attorney under the 1996 Act, it can be dealt with by the Circuit Court.

Subsections (7) and (8) mirror the provisions of s.11(3) in a limited way and s.11(5) respectively, and state that the director should supply an authenticated copy of the instrument to the attorney and the donor. The copies authenticated by the director will be evidence of the contents of the instrument and the date it came into force.

This section is wider than the corresponding provisions of s.10 of the 1996 Act concerning the registration of an enduring power. The Registrar of the Office of Wards of Court had rather limited powers under s.10, and did not have the power to refuse to register an enduring power—if there was an objection to registration, the Registrar had to await an order of the High Court. By contrast, s.69 imposes a duty on the Director to "review the application and any objections received under section 71 and shall carry out such reasonable enquiries as he or she considers necessary in order to establish" whether the criteria set out in this subsection are met. One of the criteria is whether "the attorney is a suitable person within the meaning of section 59 (6)".

If the Director refuses to register the enduring power, he or she must provide reasons and give the donor and the attorney an opportunity to respond. If the Director's view is unchanged, he or she must refuse to register the enduring power. This decision can be appealed by the attorney to the court under subs.(5).

The rather helpful provisions of s.10(5)(a) of the 1996 Act (see p.20) are not repeated here, thus limiting the power of the registrar to register an enduring power where the enduring power "differs in an immaterial respect in form of mode or expression" from the prescribed form.

Effect and proof of registration

70. (1) The effect of the registration of an instrument creating an enduring power of attorney is that—

(a) no revocation of the enduring power of attorney by the donor shall be valid unless the court confirms the revocation under section 73 (6),

(b) no disclaimer of the enduring power shall be valid except on notice to the donor and with the consent of the court, and

(c) the donor may not extend or restrict the scope of the authority conferred by him or her in the enduring power and no consent or instruction given by the donor after registration of the instrument shall, in the case of a consent, confer any right and in the case of an instruction, impose or confer any obligation or right on or create any liability of the attorney or other persons having notice of the consent or instruction.

(2) Subsection (1) applies for so long as the instrument is registered whether or not the donor has for the time being capacity.

General Note

Section 70 provides that once an instrument has been registered, a revocation of power will not be valid unless it is confirmed by the court. A disclaimer by the attorney will only be valid if it is on notice to the donor and with the consent of the court. Once registration has taken place, the donor cannot extend or restrict the power, nor can he or she give a valid consent or instruction by which the attorney will be bound. Subsection (2) provides that subs.(1) applies for so long as the instrument is registered, regardless of whether the donor lacks capacity for the time being. This section is almost identical to the provisions set out in s.11(1) and (2) of the 1996 Act.

Objections to registration

71. (1) Any of the persons referred to in section 68 (3), or any other person who appears to the Director to have sufficient interest or expertise in the welfare of the donor, may, no later than 5 weeks from the date on which notice is given in accordance with that provision, notify the Director that he or she objects to the proposed registration.

(2) An objection under subsection (1) shall be in such form and shall be accompanied by such fee as shall be prescribed by regulations made under section 79 and may be made on one or more of the following grounds:

(a) that the enduring power of attorney or instrument creating it is not in accordance with section 59, 60, 62 or 63;

(b) that the notice requirement of section 61 or section 68 (3) was not complied with;

(c) that the donor does not lack capacity;

(d) that fraud, coercion or undue influence was used to induce the donor to execute the instrument creating the enduring power of attorney;

(e) that a false statement is included in the instrument creating the enduring power of attorney or the application to register the instrument;

(f) that the attorney is not a suitable person within the meaning of section 59 (6).

(3) Where the Director receives an objection in accordance with subsection (2), made within the period specified in subsection (1), he or she shall—

(a) review the objection,

(b) consult with the attorney and, where the Director considers it is appropriate to do so, the donor, and

(c) consult with such other persons as he or she considers relevant,

and shall—

(i) where he or she is of the view that the objection is not well founded, notify the person who made the objection of his or her view, provide reasons for that view and proceed, subject to section 69 (1), to register the instrument concerned, or

(ii) where he or she is of the view that the objection is well founded, notify the person who made the objection of his or her view and make an application to the court for a determination on the matter and for a determination as to whether the enduring power should be registered.

(4) The court, pursuant to an application made to it under subsection (3) (ii), may—

(a) require the Director to register the instrument creating the enduring power of attorney,

(b) declare that the instrument creating the enduring power of attorney should not be registered, or

(c) make such other declaration or order as it considers appropriate.

(5) A person who makes an objection under subsection (1) may, not later than 21 days after the date of issue of the notification by the Director under subsection (3)(i), appeal a decision to register the instrument concerned to the court.

(6) Upon an appeal under subsection (5), the court may—

(a) require the Director to remove the instrument concerned from the Register,

(b) affirm the decision of the Director, or

(c) make such other declaration or order as it considers appropriate.

General Note

Section 71 provides that objections may be made to the registration of an instrument creating an enduring power of attorney. Subsection (1) states that any person listed in s.68(3), or any other person who appears to the Director to have sufficient interest or expertise in the welfare of the donor, may, within 5 weeks from the date on which notice is given, notify the Director that he or she objects to the registration. Section 10 of the 1996 Act, which applies to objections to registration, only appears to apply to those who have been given notice pursuant to para.2(1) of the First Schedule of the Act. Subsection (1) applying s.68(3) of the Act broadens the list of people who can object to the registration.

Subsection (2) sets out the grounds on which an objection to the registration of an instrument creating an enduring power of attorney may be made, and these are largely similar to the grounds in s.10(3) of the 1996 Act. It makes provision for objections on the grounds of false statements being included in the instrument creating the power or registering the instrument. It also refers to "coercion" to create the power. This is not referred to in the 1996 Act or the Bill. It refers to a fee being charged which according to The Minister for State at the Department of Health (Deputy Kathleen Lynch), "will help to filter out frivolous or vexatious objections" (244(6) *Seanad Éireann Debates* 9 December 2015).

Section 71 contrasts with s.10(2) to (4) of the 1996 Act (see p.20), dealing with objections to the proposed registration of an enduring power. The most important difference is that in the 1996 Act it is the High Court which is given the power to refuse an application to register an enduring power on any of the grounds of objection set out in s.10(3) of the 1996 Act, whereas under s.71(3), prior to the objection being determined by the court, the Director must review the objection, consult with the attorney and with the donor (if the Director considers this appropriate), and consult with any other persons as the Director considers relevant. After this process, the Director shall register the enduring power if he or she considers the objection not well founded (and the objector may appeal this decision to the court under subs.(5)), or apply to the court for a determination on the matter and as to whether the enduring power should be registered. Under subs.(4), the court may require the Director to register the enduring power, declare that the instrument creating the enduring power should not be registered, or make such other declaration or order as it considers appropriate. Under s.11(4) of the 1996 Act, the High Court only had the power to refuse the application to register on the grounds set out in s.11(3) of the 1996 Act.

Register of enduring powers

72. (1) The Director shall establish and maintain a register (in this Part referred to as "the Register") of instruments creating an enduring power of attorney.

(2) The Register shall be in such form as the Director considers appropriate.

(3) The Director shall make the Register available for inspection by—

(a) a body or class of persons prescribed by regulations made under section 79 for this purpose, and

(b) any person who satisfies the Director that he or she has a legitimate interest in inspecting the Register.

(4) The Director may issue an authenticated copy of an enduring power, or part thereof, on the Register on payment of the prescribed fee to—

(a) a body or class of person prescribed by regulations made under section 79 for this purpose, and

(b) a person who satisfies the Director that he or she has a legitimate interest in obtaining a copy.

(5) The Director shall keep a record of any body or person that has inspected the Register or received an authenticated copy from him or her.

General Note

Section 72 is similar to s.11(4) and (5) of the 1996 Act regarding the inspection of a register of registered enduring powers and the issuing of authenticated copies thereof, although s.72 is more detailed.

Subsections (1) and (2) require the director to establish and maintain a register of enduring powers of attorney that have been registered by him or her in such form as the Director considers appropriate.

Subsection (3) provides for inspection of the Register. The Bill as published allowed for inspection of the Register by members of the public. However, subs.(3) was amended at Committee stage in the Seanad and now the Register can only be inspected by a body or class of persons prescribed by regulations made under s.79 and any person who satisfies the Director that he or she has a legitimate interest in inspecting the Register. The Minister for State at the Department of Health (Deputy Kathleen Lynch) stated:

> "With a view to the need for data protection, particularly as enduring powers of attorney are essentially private arrangements between individuals, it is not considered appropriate to make the register open to the general public. Where it is necessary for a person or a body to know of the existence of an enduring power or to have access to some or all of its contents, the director will allow the appropriate level of access" (244(6) *Seanad Éireann Debates* 9 December 2015).

In contrast, s.11 of the 1996 Act outlines that members of the public may inspect the register free of charge during normal working hours.

Subsection (4) authorises the issuing of authenticated copies of registered enduring powers to those persons also, whereas s.11(3) restricted the issuing of attested copies to the donor and to those who were given notice of the application to register the enduring power. Subsection (5) provides for the maintaining of a record of those who have had access to the register or who have been sent an authenticated copy of an enduring power.

Revocation and variation of enduring power

73. (1) An enduring power of attorney may be varied or revoked by the donor, where the instrument creating the enduring power of attorney has not been registered and where the donor has capacity to make the variation or revocation, as the case may be.

(2) A variation or revocation under subsection (1) shall be done in such form as shall be prescribed.

(3) Subject to section 60 (3), a revocation or variation of an enduring power of attorney shall be signed by the donor and his or her signature shall be acknowledged by 2 witnesses and section 60 (4) shall apply with the necessary

modifications.

(4) A variation or revocation of an enduring power of attorney shall be accompanied by the following statements:

(a) by the donor, that he or she understands the implication of varying or revoking the enduring power, as the case may be;

(b) by a legal practitioner that, after interviewing the donor and making any necessary enquiries, he or she—

(i) is satisfied that the donor understands the implication of varying or revoking, as the case may be, the enduring power, and

(ii) has no reason to believe that the variation or revocation, as the case may be, is the result of fraud, coercion or undue pressure on the donor;

(c) by a registered medical practitioner that in his or her opinion, at the time of the variation or revocation, as the case may be, the donor had the capacity to understand the implication of the variation or revocation;

(d) by such other healthcare professional as shall be prescribed that in his or her opinion, at the time of the variation or revocation, as the case may be, the donor had the capacity to understand the implication of the variation or revocation; and

(e) by the attorney, that he or she is aware of the variation or revocation and undertakes to act accordingly.

(5) Subject to subsection (6) a donor may, after an instrument creating an enduring power of attorney has been registered, revoke the enduring power where he or she has capacity to do so.

(6) A revocation referred to in subsection (5) is not valid unless an application is made to the court and the court is satisfied that—

(a) the donor has done whatever is necessary in law to effect an express revocation of the enduring power of attorney and had capacity at the time of the purported revocation, and

(b) the donor has given notice to the attorney of the revocation.

General Note

Section 73 provides for the revocation and variation of enduring powers of attorney both before and after registration. It expands on the original section of the Bill which outlined that provision for revocation of enduring powers of attorney would be provided for by regulations. The original section did not make provision for variation of enduring powers. Where a donor has capacity, an enduring power of attorney may be varied or revoked any time prior to its registration. Subsection (2) provides that the variation or revocation must be done in such form as prescribed by the Minister. A revocation or variation shall be signed by the donor and witnessed by two people, subject to s.60(4). It also must be accompanied by the statements by the donor, legal practitioner, healthcare professional and the attorney. The corresponding section in the Bill did not require two witnesses or a statement by the attorney. Similar to the original section of the Bill, which dealt with content of instruments creating enduring powers, this original section indicated that the donor's statement must confirm that he read the information, the legal practitioner was satisfied the donor understood the effect of revoking the power, and had no reason to believe the documents was executed as a result of fraud or undue pressure. In the Bill, a separate statement was not required from a healthcare professional. It provided for a "statement by a registered medical practitioner (or other healthcare professional whom the High Court considers suitable to assess a person's capacity) that, in his or her opinion at the time the revocation was executed by the donor, the donor had the capacity, with the assistance of such explanations as may have been given to the donor, to understand the effects of revoking the power".

It is not necessary for the donor to apply to court to revoke an enduring power that has not been registered. A donor may revoke an enduring power that has been registered if he or she has the capacity to do so. However, the court must confirm the revocation for it to be valid. The 1996 Act did not make provision for the revocation of enduring powers prior to registration, although this is dealt with in the Guidelines for Solicitors set out in Appendix D at para.2.10. It is an advantage that revocation prior to registration is specifically provided for in s.73, although the requirements may seem daunting and costly. It might have been simpler to only provide that the revocation or variation of an unregistered enduring power be notified to the Director. Subsection (5) provides that a registered enduring power can only be revoked if the donor has capacity to do so, and subs.(6) goes on to provide that such revocation is not valid unless an application is made to the court and the court is satisfied that this subsection has been complied with. Subsection (6) is similar to the provisions of ss.11(1)(a) and 12(3) of the 1996 Act.

Disclaimer by attorney

74. (1) An attorney may disclaim an enduring power of attorney where the instrument creating it has not been registered subject to his or her giving notice of such disclaimer to the donor.

(2) Where an instrument creating an enduring power of attorney has been registered, the enduring power created by the instrument may only be disclaimed by an attorney with the consent of the court.

General Note

Section 74 provides that a disclaimer of an enduring power that has not been registered by the attorney will not be valid except on notice to the donor. This reflects s.5(10) of the 1996 Act. A disclaimer of an enduring power that has been registered by the attorney will not be valid except with the consent of the court. This mirrors the provisions of s.11(1)(b) of the 1996 Act.

Reports by attorney

75. (1) An attorney under an enduring power of attorney which confers authority in relation to property and affairs shall, within 3 months of the registration of the instrument appointing him or her as attorney, submit to the Director a schedule of the donor's assets and liabilities and a projected statement of the donor's income and expenditure.

(2) An attorney under an enduring power of attorney which confers authority in relation to property and affairs shall keep proper accounts and financial records in respect of the donor's income and expenditure and shall—

(a) submit such accounts and records as part of a report to the Director under this section, and

(b) make available for inspection by the Director or by a special visitor, at any reasonable time, such accounts and records.

(3) An attorney shall, within 12 months after registration of the instrument appointing him or her as attorney, and thereafter at intervals of not more than 12 months, prepare and submit to the Director a report in writing as to the performance of his or her functions as such attorney during the relevant period.

(4) Every report submitted to the Director pursuant to this section shall be in such form as shall be prescribed by regulations made under section 79 and

shall include details of all costs, expenses and remuneration paid to and claimed by the attorney in the relevant period together with such other matters as are prescribed.

(5) An attorney who has restrained the donor at any time during the relevant period shall include in the report details of each such restraint and the date on which, and the place where, such restraint occurred.

(6) Where an attorney fails to submit a report in accordance with this section or submits an incomplete report or fails to comply with subsection (1) or (2), the Director shall notify the attorney of that failure or incompleteness and give him or her such period of time as is specified in the notification to comply or submit a complete report.

(7) Where an attorney fails to comply with a notification under subsection (6), the Director shall—

(a) in the case of the submission of an incomplete report and following any necessary enquiries to satisfy himself or herself that the report is substantially in accordance with this section and regulations made under section 79, accept the report as if it were in compliance with this section and the relevant regulations, or

(b) make an application to the court for a determination as to whether the co-decision-maker should continue as attorney for the donor.

(8) Pursuant to an application to it under subsection (7)(a), the court may determine that an attorney who has not complied with this section shall no longer act as attorney for the donor concerned.

(9) In this section "relevant period" means the period of time to which the report relates which shall be the period of time between the date of registration of the instrument creating the enduring power of attorney or the date of submission of the previous report, as the case may be, and the date immediately preceding the date of submission of the report concerned.

General Note

Section 75 contains specific provision (subs.(2)) for the keeping of accounts by attorneys—a similar provision was contained in the 1996 Act—s.5(2)(e) thereof and para.5 of S.I. No. 196 of 1996. However, s.75 contains important new provisions which were not contained in the 1996 Act, providing as it does for the submission of accounts and reports in various circumstances by the attorney to the Director—subss.(1), (2), (3), (4) and (5). Subsections (6), (7) and (8) deal with the consequences of an attorney not submitting a report in accordance with this section, or submitting an incomplete report. This section is a safeguard for donor's affairs and allows for oversight of attorneys by the Director which will attempt to protect a donor from financial abuse. Subsection (1) requires an attorney who has been given the authority by the donor to make decisions on his or her property and affairs to submit within three months of the registration of the instrument creating the enduring power of attorney a schedule of the donor's assets and liabilities and projected statement of the donor's income and expenditure to the director. In relation to this section, The Minister for State at the Department of Health (Deputy Kathleen Lynch) stated:

> "This is good practice on behalf of the attorney because he or she will need to be aware of the donor's incomings and outgoings in order to effectively manage the donor's property and affairs. It also ensures the director is made aware of any substantial estates that may require closer oversight" (244(6) *Seanad Éireann Debates* 9 December 2015).

Subsection (2) places an obligation on the attorney to keep proper accounts and financial records and that such accounts and records be available for inspection by the director or special visitor and to submit them as part of their report.

Subsection (3) outlines that the attorney under a registered enduring power must submit a report as to the performance of his or her functions under the enduring power to the director within 12 months of registration, and annually thereafter. The report must also include details of any restraint used against the donor. Subsection (4) provides that reports submitted by the attorney must be in a form to be prescribed by the Minister and must include details of all expenses and remuneration paid or to be claimed by the attorney.

Subsections (6) to (8) outline the consequences for an attorney for non-compliance with his or her reporting obligations. This includes a provision that allows the court to determine that the attorney should no longer act as attorney for the donor concerned.

The Minister proposed, at Committee Stage at the Seanad, amendments which would extend the reporting obligations to attorneys of enduring powers that had been created under the 1996 Act but have not yet been registered. However, at Report stage, the Minister clarified, "I have received legal advice which sets out that imposing the new reporting obligations on attorneys who were appointed under a different law could carry constitutional risks" (244(9) *Seanad Éireann Debates* 15 December 2015).

Complaints in relation to attorneys

76. (1) A person may make a complaint in writing to the Director concerning one or more of the following matters:

(a) that an attorney has acted, is acting, or is proposing to act outside the scope of his or her functions as specified in the instrument creating the enduring power of attorney;

(b) that an attorney is not a suitable person within the meaning of section 59 (6);

(c) that fraud, coercion or undue pressure was used to induce a donor to appoint an attorney.

(2) A person may, in respect of an attorney under the Act of 1996, make a complaint in writing to the Director concerning one or more of the following matters:

(a) that an attorney under the Act of 1996, is acting or is proposing to act outside the scope of the enduring power under the Act of 1996;

(b) that an attorney under the Act of 1996 is unable, for whatever reason, to perform his or her duties and obligations as construed in accordance with that Act;

(c) that fraud, coercion or undue pressure was used to induce a donor under the Act of 1996 to appoint an attorney under the Act of 1996.

(3) Following the receipt of a complaint under subsection (1) or (2), the Director shall carry out an investigation of the matter which is the subject of that complaint and—

(a) where he or she is of the view that the complaint is well founded, make an application to the court for a determination in relation to a matter specified in the complaint, or

(b) where he or she is of the view that the complaint is not well founded, notify the person who made the complaint of that view and provide reasons for that view.

(4) A person who receives a notification under subsection (3)(b) may, not later than 21 days after the date of issue of the notification, appeal a decision of the Director that the complaint is not well founded to the court.

(5) The Director may, notwithstanding that no complaint has been received, on his or her own initiative carry out an investigation and make an application

to the court for a determination in relation to any matter specified in subsection (1) or (2).

(6) The court may—

(a) pursuant to an application to it under subsection (3)(a) or (5), or

(b) pursuant to an appeal under subsection (4),

make a determination in relation to a matter specified in subsection (1) or (2) and may, if it considers it appropriate, determine that—

(i) an attorney shall no longer act as such in relation to the donor concerned, or

(ii) an attorney under the Act of 1996 shall no longer act as such in relation to a donor under the Act of 1996.

(7) The reference to "attorney" in sections 95 and 96 shall, for the purposes of this section, be construed as including an attorney under the Act of 1996.

(8) The reference to "relevant person" in sections 95, 96 and 99 shall, for the purposes of this section, be construed as including a donor under the Act of 1996.

General Note

Section 76 sets out the procedure in relation to complaints against attorneys. Importantly, this section applies not only to attorneys appointed under the 2015 Act, but also to attorneys appointed under the 1996 Act. A person can complain if an attorney is acting or proposing to act outside the scope of his or her functions as specified in the instrument, if any attorney is an "unsuitable person" as set out in s.59(6) or if fraud, coercion or undue pressure was used to induce the donor to appoint an attorney. Subsection 3 provides that the Director shall investigate and where he or she has satisfied himself or herself that a complaint is well founded, can apply to court for a determination. Where the Director is of the view that the complaint is unfounded, he or she shall notify the person who made the complaint and provide reasons for the decision. Subsection 4 provides for an appeals procedure against the decision of the Director that the complaint is unfounded within 21 days to the courts. Subsection 5 empowers the Director to investigate a matter and make an application to court, notwithstanding that no complaint has been received. This provides a further safeguard for donors against misconduct by attorneys under both the 1996 Act and 2015 Act. The court can make a determination that an attorney, under either Act, shall no longer act as such in relation to the donor concerned.

Applications to court

77. (1) Where the Director makes an application to the court for a determination on whether the instrument creating an enduring power of attorney should be registered, the court may, notwithstanding that—

(a) the enduring power of attorney or the instrument creating it does not comply with section 59 or section 60, or

(b) the application to register the instrument was not in accordance with section 68,

register the instrument where it is satisfied that—

(i) the donor intended the power to be effective during any period when the donor lacks capacity,

(ii) fraud, coercion or undue pressure was not used to induce the donor to appoint an attorney,

(iii) the attorney is suitable within the meaning of section 59 (6) to be the donor's attorney, and

(iv) it is desirable in the interests of justice to register the enduring power.

(2) In determining whether an attorney is suitable within the meaning of section 59 (6), the court, in addition to any other matters which it considers relevant shall have regard to—

(a) the relationship and degree of connection between the donor and the attorney,

(b) the degree of involvement which will be required on the part of the attorney in the care of the donor,

(c) the willingness of the attorney to carry out his or her functions under the enduring power, and

(d) any conflict of interest which may arise.

(3) Where an instrument creating an enduring power of attorney has been registered, the court may, whether on application by the donor, the attorney, the Director or an interested party—

(a) determine any question as to the meaning or effect of the power,

(b) give directions with respect to—

(i) a relevant decision relating to the personal welfare of the donor made or about to be made by the attorney,

(ii) the management or disposal by the attorney of the property and affairs of the donor, and

(iii) the remuneration or expenses of the attorney, whether or not in default of or in accordance with any provision of the enduring power, including directions for the repayment of excessive, or the payment of additional, remuneration,

and

(c) consent to a disclaimer by the attorney of the enduring power.

(4) Where the court gives a determination under subsection (3)(a), a direction under subsection (3)(b) or a consent under subsection (3)(c), it shall cause the Director to be notified of such direction or consent and the Director shall monitor the giving of effect by the attorney to such direction or consent as the case may be.

General Note

Section 77 deals with applications to the court. Subsection (1) sets out what the court may do where the director makes an application to it in relation to whether he or she should register an instrument creating an enduring power of attorney. It mirrors the provisions of s.10(5) of the 1996 Act and confirms that the court may register an enduring power if it does not comply with s.59 and s.60 of the Act, provided it is satisfied that the criteria in subs.1(b)(I)–(IV) exist. Subsection (2) outlines the criteria that the court must take into consideration when determining if an attorney is suitable for appointment as an attorney within the meaning of s59(6).

Subsection (3) outlines that the court can determine the meaning or effect of the instrument and is similar to the provisions of s.12(2) of the 1996 Act. The court may give directions with respect to a relevant decision relating to the personal welfare of the donor made or about to be made, management or disposal by the attorney of the property, and affairs of the donor or the remuneration or expenses of the attorney and consent to a disclaimer by the attorney. Where the instrument has been registered, these applications can be brought by the donor, the attorney, the Director, or an interested party.

Subsection (4) outlines the circumstances in which the court must notify the director of its directions or determinations under subs.(3) and requires the director to monitor the giving of effect of such directions or consent by the attorney.

Removal of instrument from the Register

78. (1) The Director shall remove from the Register an instrument creating an enduring power of attorney where—

(a) there has been a revocation in accordance with section 73 (6), or

(b) subject to subsection (2), the attorney appointed under the instrument becomes disqualified.

(2) Where there is more than one attorney appointed under an enduring power of attorney or where the donor has specified a person who shall act as attorney for him or her in the event that the attorney on whom the authority is conferred dies or is unable to act or is disqualified, then in the circumstances described in subsection (1), the Director shall note on the Register in connection with the power concerned the revocation or disqualification, as the case may be.

General Note

Section 78 gives the Director power to remove from the register of enduring powers an instrument creating an enduring power where the power has been revoked or the attorney becomes disqualified, or to note on the register such fact if there is a substitute attorney appointed in the enduring power.

Regulations

79. The Minister, having regard to the requirements of this Part, shall prescribe by regulations the following matters:

(a) the form of an instrument creating an enduring power of attorney;

(b) the form of notice under section 61 of execution of an instrument creating an enduring power of attorney;

(c) the class of healthcare professionals under sections 60 (1)(d), 68 (7)(b) and 73 (4)(d);

(d) the form of application under section 68 (2) to register an instrument;

(e) the form of notice under section 68 (3) of an application to register an instrument;

(f) the form of a report under section 75 to be submitted by an attorney to the Director;

(g) the form of an objection under section 71 (2) to the registration of an instrument creating an enduring power of attorney;

(h) the form of variation or revocation under section 73 (2) of an enduring power of attorney;

(i) the bodies or classes of persons under sections 72 (3) and (4) who may inspect the Register and receive an authenticated copy of an enduring power of attorney;

(j) the fees to be paid in connection with—

(i) an application to register an enduring power of attorney,

(ii) an objection to an application to register an enduring power of attorney,

(iii) the issue of an authenticated copy of an enduring power of attorney.

General Note

Section 79 lists matters which the Minister must prescribe by Regulation, some of which are also provided for in s.5(2) of the 1996 Act. The section in the Bill which dealt with regulations was almost identical to s.5(2) of the 1996 Act. The new Regulations to be prescribed include the class of healthcare professional, the form of report to the Director, form of objection to registration, form of variation and revocation, and classes of persons who may inspect the register and receive authenticated copies of the instruments and fees. The form of statements to be executed by the donor, legal practitioner, attorney, registered medical practitioner and healthcare do not appear to be provided for in regulations, unlike the 1996 Act. Also unlike the 1996 Act, provision for execution of enduring powers of attorneys, remuneration for attorneys, attestation of signatures and provision for appointing more than one attorney are provided for in the body of the Act.

Offences in relation to enduring powers of attorney

80. (1) A person who uses fraud, coercion or undue influence to force another person to make, vary or revoke an enduring power of attorney commits an offence and shall be liable—

(a) on summary conviction, to a class A fine or imprisonment for a term not exceeding 12 months, or both, or

(b) on conviction on indictment, to a fine not exceeding €50,000 or imprisonment for a term not exceeding 5 years, or both.

(2) A person who, in an instrument creating an enduring power of attorney, in an application for registration of an enduring power of attorney, or in connection with such an application, makes a statement which he or she knows to be false in a material particular commits an offence and shall be liable—

(a) on summary conviction, to a class A fine or imprisonment for a term not exceeding 6 months, or both, or

(b) on conviction on indictment, to a fine not exceeding €15,000 or imprisonment for a term not exceeding 2 years, or both.

(3) The reference in subsection (1) to coercion or undue influence includes any case where a person's access to, or continued stay in, a designated centre or mental health facility, is contingent (whether in whole or in part) on the person having to, or being led to believe that he or she has to, create, vary or revoke an enduring power of attorney.

General Note

Section 80 provides for offenses in relation to enduring powers, some of which are also provided for in s.9(5) of the 1996 Act. It outlines that a person who uses fraud, coercion or undue influence to force another person to make, vary or revoke an enduring power will be guilty of an offence and liable on summary conviction to a fine or imprisonment for a term not exceeding 12 months, or both or on conviction on indictment, to a fine not exceeding €50,000 or imprisonment for a term not exceeding 5 years, or both. A person who makes a statement in connection with the creation or registration of instrument creating an enduring power which he or she knows to be false will also be guilty of an offence and liable on summary conviction to a fine or imprisonment for a term not exceeding 6 months or on conviction on indictment to a fine not exceeding €15,000 or imprisonment for a term not exceeding 2 years, or both.

Transitional provisions

81. (1) Subject to sections 76 (2), 76 (3), 76 (4), 76 (5), 76 (6), 76 (7) and

76 (8), this Part shall not apply to—

(a) an enduring power of attorney under the Act of 1996,

(b) an attorney under the Act of 1996, and

(c) a donor under the Act of 1996.

(2) From the date of commencement of this Part—

(a) a person shall not create an enduring power of attorney under the Act of 1996, and

(b) the Act of 1996 shall not apply to an enduring power of attorney created after that date.

General Note

Section 81 contains transitional provisions affecting the provisions of the 1996 Act. Subject to ss.76(2), 76(3), 76(4), 76(5), 76(6) and 76(8), the 2015 Act does not apply to enduring powers, attorneys or donors under the 1996 Act. However, from the commencement date, powers of attorney cannot be created under the provisions of the 1996 Act, and that Act shall not apply to enduring powers created under the 2015 Act. The effect of these provisions is that for many years there will be two different statutory regimes for enduring powers. One wonders whether it would not have been possible to create one regime for all enduring powers by, for example, providing for the registration of all enduring powers under the provisions of the 2015 Act.

ASSISTED DECISION-MAKING (CAPACITY) ACT 2015

PART 11

The purpose of this Part is to summarise Part 11 of the 2015 Act in so far as it impinges on Enduring Powers of Attorney.

Interpretation — Part 11

109. (1) In this Part—

"adult" means a person who—

(a) as a result of an impairment or insufficiency of his or her personal faculties, cannot protect his or her interests, and

(b) has reached 18 years of age;

"central authority in another Convention country" means the authority designated by that country pursuant to the Convention;

"central authority in the State" means the authority mentioned in section 113;

"Convention" means the Convention on the International Protection of Adults agreed at The Hague on 13 January 2000 (the text of which, in the English language, is for convenience of reference set out in the Schedule);

"Convention country" means a country in which the Convention is in force;

"measure" has the meaning assigned to it by section 112 (1).

(2) An expression which appears in this Part and in the Convention is to be construed in accordance with the Constitution.

(3) The High Court, court and the Director, in interpreting this Part and the Convention, may have regard to the Explanatory Report on the Convention by Mr. Paul Lagarde of 5 January 2000, edited by the Permanent Bureau of the Hague Conference on Private International Law.

General Note

Section 109 is a definition section for the purposes of this part. "Convention" is defined as the Convention on the International Protection of Adults agreed at The Hague on 13 January 2000.

Subsection (2) provides that an expression which appears both in this Part and in the Convention is to be construed in accordance with the Constitution. Subsection (3) permits the High Court, court and the Director, in interpreting this Part and the Convention, to have regard to the Explanatory Report on the Convention by Paul Lagarde of the 5 January 2000.

Convention given effect

110. This Part—

(a) gives effect in the State to the Convention in so far as this Act does not otherwise do so, and

(b) makes related provision as to the private international law of the State.

General Note

Section 110 provides that Pt 11 "gives effect in the State" to the Convention on International Protection of Adults (the "Convention") "in so far as the 2015 Act does not otherwise do so, and makes related provision as to the private international law of the State". In other words, the provisions of the Convention have the force of law in the State where the provisions of the Convention are not implemented by the 2015 Act.

Countries, territories and nationals

111. (1) In this section "country" includes a territory which has its own system of law.

(2) Where a country has more than one territory with its own system of law, a reference to the country, in relation to one of its nationals, is to the territory with which the national has the closer, or the closest, connection.

General Note

Section 111 in subs.(1) defines "country" as including a territory which has its own system of law. Subsection (2) provides that where a country has more than one territory with its own system of law, a reference to the country, in relation to one of its nationals, is to the territory with which the national in question has the closer, or the closest, connection.

Protective measures

112. (1) In this section " measure " means a measure directed to the protection of the person or property of an adult, including any of the following:

(a) the determination of incapacity and the institution of a protective regime;

(b) placing the adult under the protection of a judicial or administrative authority;

(c) guardianship, curatorship or any corresponding system;

(d) the designation and functions of a person having charge of the adult's person or property, or representing or otherwise helping him or her;

(e) placing the adult in a place where protection can be provided;

(f) administering, conserving or disposing of the adult's property;

(g) authorising a specific intervention for the protection of the person or property of the adult.

(2) Where a measure of like effect to a measure has been taken in relation to a person before he or she reached 18 years of age, this Part applies to the measure in so far as it has effect in relation to him or her once he or she has reached that age.

General Note

Section 112 defines the word "measure" as meaning a measure directed to the protection of the person or property of an adult, and therefore includes a measure taken under an enduring power of attorney.

Central authority

113. The Director is designated to perform in the State the functions conferred on the central authority in the State under this Part or by virtue of the Convention.

General Note

Section 113 provides that the Director of the Decision Support Service is designated to perform in the State the functions conferred on the central authority in the State under this Part or by virtue of the Convention.

Chapter 2

Jurisdiction of competent authority

Scope of jurisdiction

114. (1) The High Court and the court may exercise their functions under this Part (in so far as they cannot otherwise do so) in relation to—

(a) an adult habitually resident in the State,

(b) an adult's property in the State, insofar as the exercise of those functions is compatible with measures taken by the authorities of a Convention country having jurisdiction under Articles 5 to 8 of the Convention,

(c) subject to Article 10 of the Convention, an adult present in the State or who has property there, if the matter is urgent, or

(d) subject to Article 11 of the Convention, an adult present in the State, insofar as the exercise of those functions is temporary and limited to the State.

(2) An adult present in the State shall be treated for the purposes of this section and Articles 6 and 7 of the Convention as habitually resident there if—

(a) his or her habitual residence cannot be ascertained,

(b) he or she is a refugee, or

(c) he or she has been displaced as a result of disturbance in the country of his or her habitual residence.

General Note

Section 114 sets out the jurisdiction of the court (as defined in s.4 of the 2015 Act—see p.101) and the High Court (the "courts") in the exercise of their functions under this Part and generally grants jurisdiction where there is a connection with the State, such as where the adult is habitually resident in the state.

Provisions supplementary to section 114

115. (1) The High Court and the court may also exercise their functions under this Part (in so far as they cannot otherwise do so) in relation to an adult if subsection (2) or (3) applies in relation to him or her.

(2) This subsection applies in relation to an adult if—

(a) he or she is an Irish citizen, and

(b) Article 7 of the Convention has, in relation to the matter concerned, been complied with.

(3) This subsection applies in relation to an adult if the High Court or the court, as the case may be, having consulted such person as it considers appropriate, agrees to or makes a request under Article 8 of the Convention in relation to the adult.

General Note

Section 115 supplements the jurisdiction granted to the courts to include Irish citizens even if they are not resident in the State.

Exercise of jurisdiction

116. Measures taken by the High Court or the court, as the case may be, under this Part remain in force so long as the competent authorities in a Convention country have not modified, replaced or terminated such measures.

General Note

Section 116 provides that measures taken by the courts under this Part remain in force so long as they have not been affected by the competent authorities in another Convention country.

Chapter 3

Applicable law

Applicable law

117. In exercising jurisdiction under Chapter 2, the High Court or the court, as the case may be, shall apply the law of the State but may, in so far as the protection of the person or the property of the adult requires, if it thinks that the matter has a substantial connection with a country other than the State, apply or take into consideration the law of that other country.

General Note

Section 117 provides that in exercising jurisdiction the courts shall apply the law of the State but may, if it thinks that the matter has a substantial connection with a country other than the State, apply or take into consideration the law of that other country.

Provisions supplementary to section 117

118. Where a measure is taken in one Convention country but implemented in another, the conditions of implementation are governed by the law of the Convention country in which implementation occurs.

GENERAL NOTE

Section 118 provides that where a measure is taken in one Convention country but implemented in another, the conditions of implementation are governed by the law of the Convention country in which implementation occurs.

Enduring powers of attorney, etc.

119. (1) If the donor of an enduring power is habitually resident in the State at the time of granting the power, the law applicable to the existence, extent, modification or extinction of the power is—

(a) the law of the State, or

(b) if he or she specifies in writing the law of a connected country for the purpose, that law.

(2) If the donor of an enduring power is habitually resident in another country at that time, but the State is a connected country, the law applicable in that respect is—

(a) the law of the other country, or

(b) if he or she specifies in writing the law of the State for the purpose, that law.

(3) A country is connected, in relation to the donor, if it is a country—

(a) of which he or she is a national,

(b) in which he or she was habitually resident, or

(c) in which he or she has property.

(4) Where this section applies as a result of subsection (3)(c), it applies only in relation to the property which the donor has in the connected country.

(5) The law applicable to the manner of the exercise of an enduring power is the law of the country where it is exercised.

(6) In this Chapter "enduring power" means—

(a) an enduring power of attorney as provided for in section 59, or

(b) any other power of like effect.

GENERAL NOTE

Section 119 deals with enduring powers of attorney and provides that if the donor of the power is habitually resident in the State at the time the power is granted, the law relating to the existence, extent, modification or extinction of the power is the law of the State, unless the donor specifies in writing that the law of a "connected" country applies. If the donor is habitually resident in another country at that time, but the State is a "connected" country, the applicable law is the law of that other country, unless the donor specifies in writing that the law of the State applies. A connected country is defined in relation to the donor as a country of which he or she is a national, in which he or she was habitually resident, or in which he or she has property (but only in relation to that property). Subsection (5) provides that the law applicable to the exercise of an enduring power is the law of the country (not necessarily a convention country) where it is exercised. Subsection (6) provides that for the purposes of this Chapter "enduring power" means an enduring power of attorney as provided for in s.59 "or any other power of like effect".

Disapplication or modification of enduring power of attorney, etc.

120. (1) Where an enduring power is not exercised in a manner sufficient to guarantee the protection of the person or property of the donor, the High Court or the court, as the case may be, in exercising jurisdiction under this Part, may disapply or modify the power.

(2) Where, in accordance with this Chapter, the law applicable to the power is, in one or more respects, that of a country other than the State, the High Court or the court, as the case may be shall, so far as possible, take into consideration the law of the other country in that respect (or those respects).

General Note

Section 120 provides in subs.(1) that where an enduring power is not exercised in a manner sufficient to guarantee the protection of the person or property of the donor, the courts may, in exercising jurisdiction under this Part, disapply or modify the power. Subsection (2) provides that where, in accordance with this Chapter, the law applicable to the power is, "in one or more respects", that of a country other than the State, the courts shall as far as possible take into consideration the law of the other country in that respect, or those respects.

Protection of third parties

121. (1) This section applies where a person (in this section referred to as a "representative") in purported exercise of an authority to act on behalf of an adult enters into a transaction with a third party.

(2) The validity of the transaction may not be questioned in proceedings, nor may the third party be held liable, merely because—

(a) where the representative and third party are in the State when entering into the transaction,subsection (3) applies, or

(b) where they are in another country at that time,subsection (4) applies.

(3) This subsection applies if—

(a) the law applicable to the authority in one or more respects is, as a result of this Part, the law of a country other than the State, and

(b) the representative is not entitled to exercise the authority in that respect (or those respects) under the law of that other country.

(4) This subsection applies if—

(a) the law applicable to the authority in one or more respects is, as a result of this Chapter, the law of the State, and

(b) the representative is not entitled to exercise the authority in that respect (or those respects) under that law.

(5) This section shall not apply if the third party knew or ought to have known that the applicable law was—

(a) in a case within subsection (3), the law of the other country,

(b) in a case within subsection (4), the law of the State.

General Note

Section 121 deals with the protection of third parties entering into transactions with persons purporting to exercise authority to act on behalf of an adult (not just attorneys of enduring powers). Subsection (2) provides that the validity of such transactions may not be questioned in proceedings, nor may the third party be held liable, merely because where the representative and the third party are in the State, subs.(3) applies, or, where they are in another country at that time, subs.(4) applies. Subsection (3) applies if the law applicable to the authority in one or more respects is, as a result of this Part, the law of a country other than the State, and the representative is not entitled to exercise the authority in that respect (or in those respects) under the law of that other country. Subsection (4) applies if the law applicable to the authority in one or more respects is, as a result of this Chapter, the law of the State, and the representative is not entitled to exercise the authority in that respect (or in those respects) under the law of the State. However, under subs.(5), this protection does not apply if the third party knew or "ought to have known" that the applicable law was, in a case under subs.(3), the law of the other country or, in a case under subs.(4), the law of the State.

Mandatory rules

122. Where the High Court or the court, as the case may be, is entitled to exercise jurisdiction under this Part, the mandatory provisions of the law of the State apply, regardless of any system of law which would otherwise apply in relation to the matter.

General Note

Section 122 provides that where the courts are entitled to exercise jurisdiction under this Part, "the mandatory provisions of the law of the State apply", regardless of any system of law which would otherwise apply in relation to the matter.

Public policy

123. Nothing in this Part requires or enables the application in the State of a provision of the law of another country if its application would be manifestly contrary to public policy.

General Note

Section 123 provides that the law of another country is not to be applied if it is contrary to public policy (presumably Irish public policy).

Chapter 4

Recognition and enforcement

Recognition

124. (1) A measure taken in relation to an adult under the law of a Convention country other than the State is to be recognised in the State if it was taken on a ground mentioned in Chapter II (Jurisdiction) of the Convention.

(2) The High Court or the court, as the case may be, may refuse recognition of a measure if it is of the view that—

(a) the case in which the measure was taken was not urgent,
(b) the adult was not given an opportunity to be heard, and
(c) that omission amounted to a breach of natural justice.

(3) The High Court or the court, as the case may be, may refuse to recognise a measure if it is of the view that—

(a) recognition of the measure would be manifestly contrary to public policy,
(b) the measure would be inconsistent with a mandatory provision of the

law of the State, or

(c) the measure is inconsistent with one subsequently taken, or recognised, in the State in relation to the adult.

(4) The High Court or the court, as the case may be, may refuse recognition of a measure taken under the law of a Convention country other than the State in a matter to which Article 33 of the Convention applies if it is of the view that that Article has not been complied with in connection with that matter.

General Note

Section 124 deals with the recognition of measures taken in relation to an adult under the law of a Convention country other than the State, and provides in subs.(1) that such measures are to be recognised in the State if they are taken on a ground mentioned in Chapter II (jurisdiction) of the Convention. Chapter II of the Convention refers to "measures directed to the protection of the adult's person or property". Subsection (2) provides that the courts may refuse recognition of a measure if they are of the view that the case in which the measure was taken was not urgent; the adult was not given an opportunity to be heard; and that omission amounted to a breach of natural justice. Subsection (3) provides that the courts may also refuse to recognise a measure if they are of the view that recognition of the measure would be manifestly contrary to (Irish) public policy, the measure would be inconsistent with a "mandatory" provision of the law, or the measure is inconsistent with a measure subsequently taken, or recognised, in the State in relation to the adult. Finally, subs.(4) provides that the courts may refuse recognition of a measure taken under the law of a Convention country other than the State in a matter to which art.33 of the Convention applies if they are of the view that that article has not been complied with in connection with that matter. Article 33 concerns the placement of adults "in an establishment or other place where protection can be provided".

Application to High Court or court for declaration on measure

125. (1) Subject to section 124, an interested person may apply to the court for a declaration as to whether a measure taken under the law of a Convention country other than the State is to be recognised in the State.

(2) No permission is required for an application to the court under this section.

General Note

Section 125 empowers (in subs.(1)) "an interested person" to apply "to the court" for a declaration as to whether a measure taken under the law of a Convention country other than the State is to be recognised in the State, and in subs.(2) provides that no permission is required for such an application. It is noteworthy what while the title to this section refers to "High Court or court", the body of the section merely refers to "the court".

Provisions supplementary to sections 124 and 125

126. For the purposes of sections 124 and 125, any finding of fact by a competent authority in a Convention country other than the State is conclusive.

General Note

Section 126 makes a supplementary provision to ss.124 and 125—providing that for the purposes of those sections any finding of fact by a competent authority in any Convention country other than the State is conclusive.

Enforcement

127. (1) An interested person may apply to the High Court or the court for a declaration as to whether a measure taken under the law of, and enforceable in, a Convention country other than the State is enforceable in the State.

(2) The High Court or the court, as the case may be, shall make the declaration if—

(a) the measure falls within section 124 (1), and

(b) it has not refused recognition of the measure pursuant to section 124 (2), (3) or (4).

(3) A measure to which a declaration under this section relates is enforceable in the State as if it were a measure of like effect taken by the High Court or the court, as the case may be.

General Note

Section 127 deals with enforcement, providing in subs.(1) that an interested person may apply to the courts for a declaration as to whether a measure taken under the law of, and enforceable in, a Convention country other than the State is enforceable in the State. Subsection (2) provides that the courts shall make such a declaration if the measure falls within s.124(1) and recognition has not been refused pursuant to subs.(2), (3) or (4) of s.124. Subsection (3) provides that where such declaration is made, it is enforceable as if it were a measure of like effect taken by the courts.

Measures taken in relation to those aged under 18

128. (1) This Part applies to persons who have attained the age of 18 years.

(2) Where a measure was taken in respect of a person who had not attained the age of 18 years at the time the measure was taken, this Part applies to those measures insofar as the person concerned has attained the age of 18 years.

General Note

Section 128 applies this Part to measures taken when a person was under the age of 18 years insofar as that person has attained the age of 18 years.

Review of measures taken outside State

129. The High Court and the court may not review the merits of a measure taken in a Convention country other than the State except to establish whether the measure complies with this Part in so far as it is, as a result of this Part, required to do so.

General Note

Section 129 provides that the courts may not review "the merits" of a measure taken in a Convention country other than the State except to establish whether the measure complies with this Part, in so far as it is, as a result of this Part, required to do so.

Rules of court

130. Rules of court may make provision about an application under section 125 or 127.

General Note

Section 130 permits Rules of Court to make provision for applications under ss.125 and 127.

Chapter 5

Co-operation

Proposal for cross-border placement

131. (1) This section applies where it is proposed to place an adult in an establishment in a Convention country other than the State.

(2) The central authority in the State shall consult the central authority in another Convention country or other competent authority in the Convention country concerned about the proposed placement and, for that purpose, shall send it—

(a) a report on the adult, and

(b) a statement of the reasons for the proposed placement.

(3) If the central authority in another Convention country or other competent authority in the Convention country concerned opposes the proposed placement within a reasonable time, the proposed placement may not be proceeded with.

General Note

Section 131 applies where it is proposed to place an adult in an establishment in a Convention country other than the State. The Central Authority in the State shall consult with the Central Authority in the receiving state, provide certain information, and if the receiving state opposes the proposed placement, it shall not be proceeded with.

Proposal received by central authority under Article 33 of the Convention

132. A proposal received by the central authority in the State under Article 33 of the Convention in relation to an adult is to proceed unless the central authority in the State opposes it within a reasonable time.

General Note.

Section 132 provides that the State must process proposals under art.33[1] of the Convention within a reasonable time.

---

[1] Article 33:

"(1) If an authority having jurisdiction under Articles 5 to 8 contemplates the placement of the adult in an establishment or other place where protection can be provided, and if such placement is to take place in another Contracting State, it shall first consult with the Central Authority or other competent authority of the latter State. To that effect it shall transmit a report on the adult together with the reasons for the proposed placement.

(2) The decision on the placement may not be made in the requesting State if the Central Authority or other competent authority of the requested State indicates its opposition within a reasonable time."

Requests to be communicated through central authority

133. (1) Where a measure is contemplated by the High Court or the court, the central authority in the State may request the central authority in another Convention country or other competent authority in that Convention country to communicate information relevant to the protection of the adult concerned.

(2) Requests for information by a central authority in another Convention country or other competent authority in that Convention country shall be communicated through the central authority in the State.

General Note

Section 133 imposes a duty on the Central Authority of another Convention country to communicate information relevant to the protection of an adult the subject of a measure contemplated by the courts to the Central Authority of the State.

Adults in danger, etc.

134. (1) This section applies if the central authority in the State is informed that an adult—

(a) who is in serious danger, and

(b) in relation to whom the High Court or the court, as the case may be, has taken, or is considering taking, measures,

is, or has become, resident in a Convention country other than the State.

(2) The central authority in the State shall inform the central authority in another Convention country or other competent authority in that Convention country regarding—

(a) the danger, and

(a) the measures taken or under consideration.

General Note

Section 134 makes provision for the Central Authority in the State to inform the Central Authority of another Convention Country of the danger, and the proposed measures, where an adult, in relation to whom the courts are considering taking measures, is in serious danger.

Circumstances in which co-operation is prohibited

135. The central authority in the State shall not request from, or send to, a central authority in another Convention country or other competent authority in that Convention country information in accordance with Chapter V (Co-operation) of the Convention in relation to an adult if it is of the opinion that doing so—

(a) would be likely to endanger the adult or his or her property, or

(b) would amount to a serious threat to the liberty or life of a member of the adult's family.

General Note

Section 135 prohibits the Central Authority of the State from requesting from, or sending to, the central authority or other competent authority in another Convention country, information in relation to an adult which would be likely to endanger their health or property, or amount to a serious threat to the liberty or life of a member of their family.

APPENDIX TO PART 2

Selected Extracts from the Assisted Decision-Making (Capacity) Act 2015

Decision-making assistance agreement

10. (1) Subject to section 11, a person who has attained the age of 18 years and who considers that his or her capacity is in question or may shortly be in question may appoint another person who has also attained that age to assist the first-mentioned person in making one or more than one decision on the first-mentioned person's personal welfare or property and affairs, or both, in compliance with regulations made under subsection (4).

(2) An appointment as a decision-making assistant shall be made in a decision-making assistance agreement which is in compliance with regulations made under subsection (4).

(3) A decision-making assistance agreement may be revoked by the appointer or by the decision-making assistant at any time and, subject to agreement between the appointer and the decision-making assistant, may be varied at any time.

(4) The Minister shall make regulations as respects decision-making assistance agreements, including—

- (a) prescribing the form of a decision-making assistance agreement,
- (b) prescribing procedures and requirements relating to the execution, variation and revocation of a decision-making assistance agreement,
- (c) prescribing information to be included in or annexed to a decision-making assistance agreement for the purpose of ensuring that any document purporting to create a decision-making assistance agreement incorporates adequate information as to the effect of making or accepting the appointment,
- (d) providing for the inclusion in a decision-making assistance agreement of the following statements:
  - (i) by the appointer, that he or she has read and understands the information as to the effect of making the appointment or that such information has been explained to the appointer, by a person other than the proposed decision-making assistant; and
  - (ii) by the decision-making assistant, that he or she understands and undertakes to act in accordance with the functions of a decision-making assistant, including the duty to act in accordance with the guiding principles,
- (e) specifying the personal welfare or property and affairs, or both, which may be specified in a decision-making assistance agreement,
- (f) providing for the attestation of the signatures of the appointer and decision-making assistant by a person other than the appointer or the proposed decision-making assistant, and
- (g) the giving by the appointer of notice of the execution, variation or revocation of a decision-making assistance agreement—
  - (i) to the Director, and
  - (ii) to other specified persons, and whether or not by reference to persons who, under this Act, are required to be notified of an

application made under this Act.

(5) An appointer may, in the decision-making assistance agreement, appoint more than one person as a decision-making assistant and may specify that the decision-making assistants shall act—

(a) jointly,

(b) jointly and severally, or

(c) jointly in respect of some matters and jointly and severally in respect of other matters.

Co-decision-making agreement

17. (1) Subject to the provisions of this section and section 18, a person who has attained the age of 18 years and who considers that his or her capacity is in question or may shortly be in question may appoint a suitable person who has also attained that age to jointly make with the first-mentioned person one or more than one decision on the first-mentioned person's personal welfare or property and affairs, or both, in compliance with this Part and regulations made under section 31.

(2) A person is suitable for appointment as a co-decision-maker if he or she—

(a) is a relative or friend of the appointer who has had such personal contact with the appointer over such period of time that a relationship of trust exists between them, and

(b) is able to perform his or her functions under the co-decision-making agreement.

(3) An appointment as a co-decision-maker shall be made in writing in a co-decision-making agreement that is in compliance with this section and regulations made under section 31.

(4) Notwithstanding the definition of "property and affairs" in section 2 an appointer shall not include in a co-decision-making agreement provision for the disposal of his or her property by way of gift.

(5) A co-decision-making agreement shall contain the following:

(a) the name, date of birth and contact details of the appointer;

(b) subject to subsection (6), the signature of the appointer and the date that he or she signed the agreement;

(c) the name, date of birth and contact details of the co-decision-maker;

(d) the signature of the co-decision-maker and the date that he or she signed the agreement;

(e) the signatures of the 2 witnesses referred to in subsection (7)(a).

(6) A co-decision-making agreement may be signed on behalf of the appointer by a person who has attained the age of 18 years and who is not the co-decision-maker or one of the witnesses referred to in subsection (7)(a) if—

(a) the appointer is unable to sign the agreement,

(b) the appointer is present and directs that the agreement be signed on his or her behalf by that person, and

(c) the signature of the person is witnessed in accordance with subsection (7)(b).

(7)(a) The appointer, or the person signing on his or her behalf in accordance with subsection (6), and the co-decision-maker shall sign the co-decision-making agreement in the presence of each other and in the presence of 2 witnesses—

(i) each of whom has attained the age of 18 years,

(ii) of whom at least one is not an immediate family member of the appointer or the co-decision-maker, and

(iii) neither of whom is an employee or agent of the co-decision-maker.

(b) Each of the witnesses referred to in paragraph (a) shall witness the signature of the appointer, or the person signing on his or her behalf, and the signature of the co-decision-maker by applying his or her own signature to the co-decision-making agreement.

(8) An appointer may appoint more than one person as a co-decision-maker but may not—

(a) appoint in the same co-decision-making agreement more than one person as a co-decision-maker, or

(b) appoint in a co-decision-making agreement a co-decision-maker in respect of a relevant decision which is the subject of another co-decision-making agreement.

(9) The Director shall, on a request being made of him or her by a person who intends to appoint a co-decision-maker or a person who is proposed as a co-decision-maker, or both, provide information to the person requesting with regard to making and entering into the co-decision-making agreement.

(10) In this section, "immediate family member" means—

(a) a spouse, civil partner, or cohabitant,

(b) a child, son-in-law or daughter-in-law,

(c) a parent, step-parent, mother-in-law or father-in-law,

(d) a brother, sister, step-brother, step-sister, brother-in-law or sister-in-law,

(e) a grandparent or grandchild,

(f) an aunt or uncle, or

(g) a nephew or niece.

Offences in relation to co-decision-making agreements

34. (1) A person who uses fraud, coercion or undue influence to force another person to make, vary or revoke a co-decision-making agreement commits an offence and shall be liable—

(a) on summary conviction, to a class A fine or imprisonment for a term not exceeding 12 months, or both, or

(b) on conviction on indictment, to a fine not exceeding €50,000 or imprisonment for a term not exceeding 5 years, or both.

(2) A person who, in an application for registration of a co-decision-making agreement, or in connection with such an application, makes a statement which he or she knows to be false in a material particular commits an offence and shall be liable—

(a) on summary conviction, to a class A fine or imprisonment for a term not exceeding 6 months, or both, or

(b) on conviction on indictment, to a fine not exceeding €15,000 or imprisonment for a term not exceeding 2 years, or both.

(3) The reference in subsection (1) to coercion or undue influence includes

any case where a person's access to, or continued stay in, a designated centre or mental health facility, is contingent (whether in whole or in part) on the person having to, or being led to believe that he or she has to, make, vary or revoke a co-decision-making agreement.

Power of court to make declarations as to capacity, etc.

37. (1) The court, on application to it by a person entitled by virtue of section 36 to make the application, may make one or both of the following declarations:

(a) a declaration that the relevant person the subject of the application lacks capacity, unless the assistance of a suitable person as a co-decision-maker is made available to him or her, to make one or more than one decision specified in the declaration relating to his or her personal welfare or property and affairs, or both;

(b) a declaration that the relevant person the subject of the application lacks capacity, even if the assistance of a suitable person as a co-decision-maker were made available to him or her, to make one or more than one decision specified in the declaration relating to his or her personal welfare or property and affairs, or both.

(2) Where the court makes a declaration pursuant to subsection (1)(a), it shall, unless it is clear to the court at that time that the relevant person does not intend to enter into a co-decision-making agreement, allow the relevant person such period of time as the court considers necessary (and taking account of the time periods set out in Part 4) to register a co-decision-making agreement.

(3) Subject to subsection (4), the court, on application to it by a person entitled by virtue of section 36 to make the application, may make a declaration as to the lawfulness of an intervention proposed to be made in respect of the relevant person the subject of the application.

(4) Subsection (3) shall not apply to an intervention where—

(a) the intervener is the court or High Court, or

(b) the intervention is being taken pursuant to an order made, or a direction given, under this Act by the court or High Court

Offences in relation to advance healthcare directives

90. (1) A person who uses fraud, coercion or undue influence to force another person to make, alter or revoke an advance healthcare directive commits an offence and shall be liable—

(a) on summary conviction, to a class A fine or imprisonment for a term not exceeding 12 months, or both, or

(b) on conviction on indictment, to a fine not exceeding €50,000 or imprisonment for a term not exceeding 5 years, or both.

(2) A person who knowingly creates, falsifies or alters, or purports to revoke, an advance healthcare directive on behalf of another person without that other person's consent in writing when the other person has the capacity to do so commits an offence and shall be liable—

(a) on summary conviction, to a class A fine or imprisonment for a term not exceeding 12 months, or both, or

(b) on conviction on indictment, to a fine not exceeding €50,000 or imprisonment for a term not exceeding 5 years, or both.

(3) The reference in subsection (1) to coercion or undue influence includes any case where a person's access to, or continued stay in, a designated centre or mental health facility is contingent (whether in whole or in part) on the person having to, or being led to believe that he or she has to, make, alter or revoke an advance healthcare directive.

Offence of ill-treatment or wilful neglect

145. A decision-making assistant, co-decision-maker, decision-making representative, attorney for the relevant person, or designated healthcare representative who ill-treats or wilfully neglects the relevant person shall be guilty of an offence and shall be liable—

(a) on summary conviction, to a class A fine and imprisonment for a term not exceeding 12 months, or both, or

(b) on conviction on indictment, to a fine not exceeding €50,000 or imprisonment for a term not exceeding 5 years, or both.

Index